T0132172

# THE HEALTHY FINANCIALS FORMULA

*The Essential Guide to Improve
Your True Personal Wealth*

First Edition

GEE GACHELIN

BALBOA.
PRESS
A DIVISION OF HAY HOUSE

Copyright © 2018 Gee Gachelin.

All rights reserved. No part of this book may be used or reproduced by any means, graphic, electronic, or mechanical, including photocopying, recording, taping or by any information storage retrieval system without the written permission of the author except in the case of brief quotations embodied in critical articles and reviews.

Balboa Press books may be ordered through booksellers or by contacting:

Balboa Press
A Division of Hay House
1663 Liberty Drive
Bloomington, IN 47403
www.balboapress.com
1 (877) 407-4847

Because of the dynamic nature of the Internet, any web addresses or links contained in this book may have changed since publication and may no longer be valid. The views expressed in this work are solely those of the author and do not necessarily reflect the views of the publisher, and the publisher hereby disclaims any responsibility for them.

The author of this book does not dispense medical advice or prescribe the use of any technique as a form of treatment for physical, emotional, or medical problems without the advice of a physician, either directly or indirectly. The intent of the author is only to offer information of a general nature to help you in your quest for emotional and spiritual well-being. In the event you use any of the information in this book for yourself, which is your constitutional right, the author and the publisher assume no responsibility for your actions.

Any people depicted in stock imagery provided by Thinkstock are models, and such images are being used for illustrative purposes only.
Certain stock imagery © Thinkstock.

Print information available on the last page.

ISBN: 978-1-5043-9588-5 (sc)
ISBN: 978-1-5043-9590-8 (hc)
ISBN: 978-1-5043-9589-2 (e)

Library of Congress Control Number: 2018901238

Balboa Press rev. date: 01/26/2018

Scripture taken from the Holy Bible, NEW INTERNATIONAL VERSION®. Copyright © 1973, 1978, 1984, 2011 by Biblica, Inc. All rights reserved worldwide. Used by permission. NEW INTERNATIONAL VERSION® and NIV® are registered trademarks of Biblica, Inc. Use of either trademark for the offering of goods or services requires the prior written consent of Biblica US, Inc.

Scripture taken from the King James Version of the Bible.

Scripture taken from the New King James Version. Copyright © 1979, 1980, 1982 by Thomas Nelson, Inc. Used by permission. All rights reserved.

# CONTENTS

# Contents

# ACKNOWLEDGEMENTS

It took me over two years to write this book and I want to say a big "thank you" to everyone who actively participated in the production process, from editing all the way to the back cover design.

I am truly grateful to all the professionals who took time to give an experienced and professional testimony.

I also want to say thank you to my family and friends, co-workers and employees who impacted my life and who helped me become the person I am today.

And finally I want to say a *very special thank you to all my clients and business associates that entrusted me and referred me to others.*

*Gee*

# INTRODUCTION

My name is Gee Gachelin; I am an accountant and network marketer for a nutrition company.

After graduating from college in 2007, I started working full time as a staff accountant for a real estate company. Soon thereafter, I opened my own accounting consulting business. A couple of years later I was drawn into a nutritional network marketing company that promotes better nutrition, health, vitality, and overall wellness. About the same time, I discovered the great economic value in network marketing and recognized a tremendous opportunity to further help my clients by offering my accounting, bookkeeping, and tax consulting services.

That is when my company, Healthy Financials Inc., was born. My goal has been and continues to be to help as many people as possible to improve their health and finances.

Helping others through their health and financial challenges has become a deep passion of mine. Along the way, I have assisted hundreds of clients in overcoming difficulties in these important areas of life. This is attested by my company's customer loyalty and satisfaction.

The more I interact with clients, the more I am convinced that health and finances impact every single area of life.

Please take a look at the following graph:

## YOUR
## INPUT
## AFFECTS

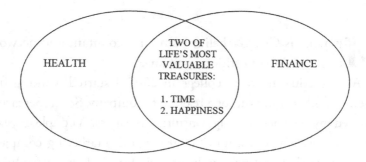

Consequentially, I have come to the following realization:

Your input toward your health and finances will considerably affect "two of life's most valuable treasures," which are: 1) Time and 2) Happiness.

## Time

Why is time so important? The answer is simple; because time is limited. In a subsequent chapter dealing with finances, I will re-emphasize this point.

You only have one life to live and how you spend it is crucial. You may work long hours to buy all the newest styles of shoes, and you may have a full closet. But the truth is, you can have dozens or even hundreds of shoes, but you will always have only one life. If you manage your time properly, you open up your world to travel, career changes, business ventures, time spent with family and friends, rest, play and much more. Whatever "floats your boat" can be yours if you manage your time properly.

# Happiness

We are not guaranteed happiness, but obtaining inner *joy and peace* is a benchmark of happiness. Where does your definition of success lie? This is where you will find your happiness. Happiness is not *obtained* or *bought,* but *chosen.* We choose to be happy, just as we choose to live in financial freedom and more nutritionally. Go to any library and you will find hundreds of books on health and hundreds more on finances. A quick internet search will produce more results on these subjects than you could read in a lifetime. But you would be hard-pressed to find information anywhere that would offer help for both your health *and* finances.

I admit, either subject is massive on its own. But, in my opinion, it's important to address these topics in order to live a full and satisfied life.

On the health side, the United States is not doing well—obesity is reaching sky-high levels, thousands of people are dying from cancer each year, and cardiovascular diseases are the #1 killer.

On the financial side, the average household owes more than $7,000 in credit card debt and 40% of working-Americans are not saving for retirement.

I took the initiative to write this book in order to help as any people as possible. I hope you will find this book insightful, inspirational, and helpful. And, if you do find this book valuable, please recommend it to someone else so they too can improve their health and finances.

# CHAPTER 1

# THE BEGINNING PROCESS

Life is hectic. Sometimes it's easy to miss the simple steps we should take before embarking on a new project, or those things we should do in the beginning of our daily routine.

For example, sometimes we forget:

- ➤ To stretch before exercising.
- ➤ To check weather and traffic reports before leaving the house.
- ➤ To make a shopping list before going to the grocery store.
- ➤ To pack a first aid kit before traveling.
- ➤ To read the educational materials before attending classes.

There is no difference when it comes to our health and personal finances. To attain proper health and become and *remain* financially fit, there are steps we must follow from the beginning.

Regardless of your belief in God, one incontrovertible fact remains, the Bible is the most printed book in the world, with over 5 to 6 billion copies in print. This being said, there are a few interesting points worth noting in the first sentence of the first book in the Bible:

*"In the beginning God created the heavens and the earth"* (Genesis 1:1 KJV).

Wow! How interesting.

Notice the fifth word, which is also the first verb of the Bible: *created.* Creating requires thought, imagination, and invention in order to produce something unique.

Why do I reference the first sentence in the Bible? Simply because if God, as a supreme and perfect being, starts His ultimate project by the process of creation, shouldn't that be a source of inspiration for us? Is it possible for us to create good health and good financial management systems *from the beginning* just as God created the heavens and the earth in the beginning?

The first sentence in the Bible could be a tremendous source of inspiration and insight for all of us.

By the same token, it is equally important to note what is *absent* from the first sentence in the Bible. Nowhere does it say:

> In the beginning God **WORKED**.
> In the beginning God **PAID**.
> In the beginning God **READ**.

Is it safe, therefore, to say that good health and proper finances can be *created* from the beginning of our life's journey? I personally believe that it's both possible *and* feasible.

As individuals, we have a chance to create, to fashion and design a lifestyle and habits that result in good health and good financial standing.

To create good health and good finances, there are two simple yet powerful steps to follow:

1. Identify the things we do *not* want, thus ensuring these negatives do not emerge in the future.
2. Identify the things we would like to have. This will keep us focused and satisfied.

We are basically creating an image of who we would like to be and the life we would like to have.

Let's start with our health. Here are some of the diseases and health issues—all painful, devastating, and agonizing—that we should strive to stay away from:

➢ Cardiovascular disease
➢ Cancer
➢ Diabetes
➢ Chronic pain
➢ Stress
➢ Obesity

Now, let's look at the qualities we *desire* for our health:

➢ Energy
➢ Vigor
➢ Longevity
➢ Pain-free living
➢ Resiliency
➢ Tenacity

When it comes to finances, we can all identify negative and unpleasant conditions we would like to improve. To put it bluntly, it's not fun being poor, struggling day to day to make ends meet.

Here are the financial conditions we want to avoid:

➢ Being broke.
➢ Working paycheck to paycheck.
➢ Owing money to creditors, family, and/or friends.
➢ Living in an undesirable and/or dangerous neighborhood.
➢ Lacking an emergency fund.
➢ Compromising your integrity due to financial difficulties.

Now, let's look at the financial conditions we should desire:

➢ Having an emergency fund.
➢ Earning residual or surplus money without having to work every day.
➢ Living in a safe and pleasant neighborhood.
➢ Having enough money to invest without stressing over simple things.
➢ Eliminating debt and living without fear of losing your assets.
➢ Indulging in occasional luxury without remorse or regret.
➢ Being in a position to help others financially.

Now that we have covered "the beginning," (which is knowing what we want vs. what we don't want), let's get ready to jump into our next topic: the "PLEASE HELP" acronym.

5

THE FIRST HALF OF YOUR "PERSONAL WEALTH" SHOULD GO TOWARDS YOUR SPIRITUAL, MENTAL AND PHYSICAL HEALTH. THE SECOND HALF SHOULD BE PRIMARILY DOMINATED BY YOUR FINANCES, FOLLOWED BY WAT YOU PERSONALLY DEFINE.

*Guitry Gachelin*

# "TRUE PERSONAL WEALTH"

It's simply defined as an abundance of the following
important possessions allocated accordingly:

50% towards your personal HEALTH

35% towards your personal FINANCES

$+$ 15% towards what you personally DEFINE

---

**100%** "TRUE PERSONAL WEALTH"

# CHAPTER 2

# THE "PLEASE HELP" ACRONYM

The PLEASE HELP acronym is "The Healthy Financials Formula," which is the central theme and heart of this book. It's important to pay attention to this formula, understand it, and work diligently on each letter. I believe this acronym is universal, but as it applies to your individual health and finances, it can make a measurable difference in your life.

When using the PLEASE HELP acronym, it is vital that we are consider the following:

1. Pitfalls to avoid
2. Success formula to obtain

No matter where you are in life, even if you are already successful, using the PLEASE HELP acronym can help you improve certain areas of your health and finances. PLEASE HELP stands for:

**PHILOSOPHY:** Your personal philosophy is the mental thoughts and belief systems that engage your actions.

**LAWS IN PLACE:** Physical laws state that a particular phenomenon always occurs if certain conditions are present.

**ESTIMATE THE COST:** An outlay or expenditure of money, time, labor, trouble, sweat, and hardships required to acquire, produce, accomplish, or maintain anything.

**ATTITUDE:** Mental reaction toward something. Also, an attitude can be defined as a positive or negative evaluation of people, objects, events, activities, ideas, or just about anything in your environment.

**SOURCE AND RESOURCES:** A source is anything or any place from which something comes, arises, or is obtained. Resources are a source of supply, support, or aid, especially those that can be readily drawn upon when needed.

**EFFECTIVE TIME MANAGEMENT:** Time management is the act or process of planning and exercising conscious control over the amount of time spent on specific activities, especially to increase effectiveness, efficiency, or productivity.

**HAVING A PLAN:** A plan is simply a list of all of the steps, with timing and resources, needed to achieve an objective or a desired goal.

**EVALUATE:** Determination of a subject's merit, worth, and significance, using criteria governed by a set of standards.

**LEARN THE FUNDAMENTALS:** Serving as a basis for supporting the existence of something. In other words, a fundamental is an essential part or the foundation of a structure.

**PRACTICE DISCIPLINES:** Disciplines are activities, exercises, or regimens that develop or improve the outcome of something worth attaining.

The PLEASE HELP acronym is massive and colossal. Do not take it lightly because the acronym, if applied correctly, can cause radical and tremendous change in your life.

With the definition of PLEASE HELP in place, let's gather some information regarding health and finances. Then, we will come back to the acronym and apply its individual elements.

# CHAPTER 3

# MENTAL TOUGHNESS

Like so many things in life, the state of your health and finances depends on how much effort you put into them. The results depend on the effort, sacrifices, sweat, and labor you invest into improving. But these results also correlate with your mental toughness. The tougher you are mentally, the better you will be able to tackle health and financial matters. With the right tools, philosophies, and surroundings, you will strengthen your capacity to resist temptation and achieve desirable results.

Mental toughness is probably one of the most important topics we will cover. If your mental strength is properly guided, it can produce some fascinating and amazing results. Mental toughness is a good metric to identify the good from the average and the poor.

I have identified four important components of mental toughness that I believe are the pillars (characteristics) upon which mental toughness relies upon:

➤ Extreme Desires
➤ Proper Perceptions
➤ Positive Attitude
➤ Personality Attributes

Let's examine each one of these pillars in detail:

### Extreme Desires

Extreme desires can be broken down into two parts: negative and positive.

- **Negative**

"Enough is enough; I don't want to make the same mistake again. The last one cost me too much. I got burned. I cried. I have been slain and violated. I greatly suffered. That experience left a bitter taste in my mouth. I was living in hell where darkness reigned over me with no foreseeable light of exit. Pure evil and wickedness were in control." Sounds bad, right? Yet, out of all of the previous sayings, extreme desire *can be* created and developed.

- **Positive**

"I want this. I will work night and day toward this goal. I cannot imagine another day without _____. I cannot wait to get this. I really love spending time doing _____. I get butterflies when I _____. Life is too short for me to miss _____. I was born to do _____. I would bet my life over _____. I have a burning desire that has no limit. I will do it or die trying. I am going to the 'Promised Land.' I will fight until my last breath."

Sounds energetic, motivating, and purposeful. Out of all of the previous sayings, extreme desire *can be* created and developed.

## Proper Perceptions

Mental toughness is based upon our perception regarding an object, event, person, etc. As we read earlier, mental toughness depends mostly on our history but, more importantly, on how we interpret it. For example, let's pretend you were in a loving and stable relationship for three years. One morning, to your surprise, you learn that your partner had an affair. Here are potential reactions:

➢ I will never trust a partner again and never get married.
➢ All men are unfaithful (or all women have skeletons in their closets).
➢ I forgive you, but our relationship is over. I will make sure next time to have better judgment before choosing someone as my partner.

Your reaction to any situation will depend on your conditioning: in other words, your education, beliefs, and experiences accumulated with time. In this regard, I believe that having the right mental outlook will help produce great results and make you tougher mentally as well. Another aspect of mental toughness is being able to envision the end goal. There is a great book by Stephen Covey called *"The Seven Habits of Highly Effective People"* that clearly illustrates this point. If you are able to see your current hardship as temporary and as a necessary step to accomplish spectacular results, you will become tougher mentally, and you will not get discouraged by adversities and the blowing of the wind. But this is up to *you*. *You* will have to picture a brighter future and say to yourself during times of hardship, "I am only passing through this hardship in order for me to get better."

Our final aspect of perception is having faith. Regardless of your religious beliefs, a good definition of *faith* is found in the Holy Bible: *"Faith is the substance of things hoped for, the evidence of things not seen"* (Hebrews 11:1 NIV).

Living by faith is very much different from living by sight. Allow me to quote from two other biblical verses that will help change your perception and build your mental strength: *"And we know that in all things God works for the good of those who love him"* (Romans 8:28 NIV), and *"What, then, shall we say in response to these things? If God is for us, who can be against us?"* (Romans 8:31 NIV).

To properly illustrate these points regarding faith, if something we consider bad is happening to us, we need to see the hands of a loving God behind our current situation as a:

➤ Change of course direction
➤ Disciplinary action
➤ Blessing
➤ Lesson

## Positive Attitude

Your attitude is expressed by the words that come out of your mouth and your body language.

How is positive attitude related to mental toughness? By being bold and taking action. For instance, if you want your health to improve, be bold and join a gym or participate in an outdoor sporting event. If you want more money, you need to start doing something to generate income (work, buy & sell, create, manufacture, etc.).

Taking the first step is hard, but that's what builds mental toughness. Being bold and taking action.

Mental toughness is all about having a positive attitude that focuses on your strength and the things you know instead of your weaknesses and things you don't know. For example if I am playing basketball with someone younger than me, I will focus on my experience and my wisdom to beat him. I will not focus on the fact that he's younger and maybe faster or more agile than me.

Part of a good and positive attitude is self-control. When the road is dark and the path is unclear, when someone is cursing at you or discouraging you, yet you are still able to maintain your calm and confidence and resist the temptation of cursing and yelling —then, you have self-control. That type of positive attitude creates mental toughness. We have all heard negative words from other people that provoke within us burning anger. But keeping calm shows a deep level of mental toughness.

## Personality Attributes

Personality is of great importance, especially when it comes to mental toughness. Through experiences, social contacts, and maturity we develop a unique personality and, hopefully, in our accumulation of personality traits, we capture all the ingredients necessary to develop a tough personality. Here are attributes I believe make us mentally tough:

- **Purpose-driven**

Someone who is purpose-driven is confident and focused. They have the mentality of, "I will do it or I will die." By nature, they are competitive and they cannot be easily stopped. Such power and strength makes that individual mentally tough.

- **Sense of Being Unique and Special**

By nature, every human is unique and every human has different DNA and a unique set of fingerprints. But the reality is that not everybody embraces that uniqueness. Feeling unique and special creates that sense of genuine power that eventually turns into mental toughness.

- **Integrity**

In itself, having integrity makes you strong and tough. This is because with integrity comes a clear conscience. With integrity, you are able to delight in yourself.

Hopefully you will be able to memorize and grasp the pillars of mental toughness:

- ➢ Extreme Desires
- ➢ Proper Perceptions
- ➢ Positive Attitude
- ➢ Personality Attributes

Because if you are tough mentally a lot of doors will open for you in the future and you will be able to better enjoy life.

Now that we've discussed mental toughness, which is a prerequisite to being physically and financially fit, let's go into the elements of good health.

# CHAPTER 4

# ELEMENTS OF GOOD HEALTH

To stay in good shape you must first appreciate your health. That sense of appreciation and knowing the value of your health will increase your level of care for your body. Maybe you've been ill in the past or watched a family member suffer from a chronic disease, and that became a wake-up call for you. Or you might be someone like me who's naturally passionate about good health and feeling good. Whatever your story, I am glad that you now have the motivation to get better and feel better.

There are hundreds, even thousands, of books regarding health and wellness. The objective of *this* book is to keep it short, simple, and on point while remaining effective. Since I have read books and taken different classes, I have been able to identify the following 6 elements of good health:

1. Nutrition
2. Exercise
3. Water
4. Detox / Tune-up and Maintenance
5. Supplements
6. Rest

Before digging into each of these, here is an example of the approximate values the average healthy human body should consist of:

➢ 65% water
➢ 20% fat
➢ 10% protein
➢ 5% minerals

Most diseases and disorders are related to abnormal body composition or changes in body composition. *That's it.* The most common disease is obesity, which leads to heart failure, diabetes, high cholesterol, joint pain, and so much more. Therefore, maintaining the proper balance in your body composition is crucial.

The number of cells that make up the human body ranges from about 5 trillion to 50 trillion. That's a lot of cells. But what is a cell? A *cell* is the basic structural and functional unit of all known living organisms. It is the smallest unit of life that is classified as a living thing, and is often called the "building block of life."

The world has less than 10 billion people and our body has more than 1000 times that in cells. When we talk about the world, we often mention "peace and harmony." I don't think it's that much different with the human body. If we don't guard it and keep it safe from intruders and war creators (viruses, pollutants, etc.) catastrophes will occur.

So let's look at some key ingredients in guarding our bodies:

## 1. Nutrition

High performance requires premium fuel. For example, a high performance car or motorcycle won't perform properly if you put regular gas in it. Likewise, a high performance athlete won't perform well while eating pizza and cheeseburgers all day long. Keep this in mind as we move forward. In the next chapter, we will discuss more about the necessary nutrition our body requires in order to perform well.

## 2. Exercise

Do not underestimate the importance of exercise. Our bodies are finite. Eventually, flesh and blood will pass away. This is a reality we all have to live with.

When I speak of exercise, I am referring to the following:
- Strength Training (lifting weights)
- Cardiovascular Conditioning (running, cycling, etc.)
- Flexibility Training (stretching, yoga, etc.)

Let's look at the immediate and direct effects of these three. Direct benefits of …

➢ Strength TrainingIncreases strength and power
- Increases lean body mass
- Increases ligaments and tendon tensile strength
- Boosts metabolic rate by up to 15%

➢ Cardiovascular Conditioning
- Increases oxygen intake
- Increases cardiac output and efficiency (enables the heart to function properly)
- Improves stamina (physical and psychological strength to resist or withstand illness, fatigue)
- Improves lung-heart capacity

➢ Flexibility TrainingImproves range of motion
- Improves posture
- Reduces risk of injury
- Improves balance

As important (if not more important) as the direct benefits of exercise, are the indirect benefits.

Some indirect benefits of exercise are …
- An increase in nitric oxide levels
- Improvement in blood circulation
- Reduction in blood pressure
- Improvement in insulin utilization; reduces Type II Diabetes
- Weight control
- An increase in energy
- An increase in HDL (good cholesterol)
- An improvement in digestion and elimination
- Lessening or elimination of depression
- An improvement in sexual performance

- Mood elevation
- A delay or prevention in cellular aging
- Prevention from many forms of cancers
- Reduction in the risk of osteoarthritis
- An improvement in neuromuscular coordination and balance
- An enhancement in immune system and disease resistance
- An enhancement in body power and speed
- Reduction in stress levels
- An improvement in concentration and mental function
- Better sleep
- A reduction in anxiety
- A sense of wellbeing

As you can see, the indirect benefits of exercise could easily be more important than the direct benefits.

My recommendation is that you exercise at least three times a week. DO NOT MAKE THIS OPTIONAL. Skipping out on exercise means inviting problems into your body and into your life. Whether you go to the gym, to a park, or exercise at home, make sure to include exercise in your weekly schedule. While you exercise, keep in mind the 22 indirect benefits of exercising listed above.

### 3. Drinking Water

Drinking sufficient water is not optional. Remember, the body is 60 to 70% water. Therefore it's crucial to replenish your body with fresh cold clean water. You can survive weeks without food, but only a few days without water.

*Water is life.*

Don't think any other beverages are a replacement for water. You may say, "I don't like water, but I drink plenty of juice, soda, coffee, tea …" This is not the same as drinking water. Drinking soda, coffee, or tea actually causes more water loss than the amount of water they contain, resulting in a net loss of water, or dehydration.

Dehydration causes the following:

➢ Fatigue
➢ Constipation
➢ Headache
➢ Indigestion
➢ Muscle and joint aches and pains
➢ Asthma
➢ Allergies
➢ High blood pressure
➢ Depression
➢ Diabetes
➢ Strokes
➢ High cholesterol
➢ Tinnitus
➢ Hearing loss
➢ Glaucoma
➢ Cataracts
➢ And much more …

A formula for figuring out the amount of water your body needs daily is to drink as many ounces of water equal to half of what your body weighs in pounds. For example, let's say you weigh 200 pounds; you should drink 100 ounces (or 12 ½ cups) of water per day.

I keep 1.5 liters of water with me at all times. And I make sure I drink it every day. You can do this too, based on your weight.

Another recommendation is to drink *before* eating (not while eating) so that you will eat less and keep your body hydrated.

Drinking water has many advantages, including:

➤ Increases metabolic rate
➤ Increases energy
➤ Keeps your skin young and beautiful
➤ Helps you eliminate toxins
➤ Helps you avoid all the items on the previous list
➤ Transports nutrients and oxygen throughout your body
➤ Regulates body temperature
➤ Helps with weight loss
➤ Helps to avoid other complications

## 4. Detox/ Tune-up and Maintenance

To understand this section better I am going to use a car as an analogy. Both a car and the body require fuel (for the car, gasoline; for the body, food), fluids (for the car, water, coolants, etc.; for the body, vitamins), pumps (in a car, fuel pumps, etc.; in the body, the heart), lubricants (in the car, motor oil; in the body, Omega3, which is good for joints) and electric sparks (in the car, this is a necessary mechanism that allows the engine to work; in the body, these sparks come from the brain).

Whenever a car is not performing well, we take it to the mechanic. Many people take their cars in only when the maintenance light shows up on the dash, indicating a problem. Some only take them when the problems have gotten so bad that their car is incapable of taking them from Point A to Point B. Others go routinely for an oil change, to replace spark plugs, to have their tires rotated, to change the filters (oil, air, gas). This way their car performs well for as long as possible.

Sadly, we don't have a light that shows up on our "dashboard," telling us to go to a doctor, nutritionist, chiropractor, etc. Most people wait until they are sick before doing some maintenance or preventive care.

So, let's talk about the "tune up" and "maintenance" necessary for our bodies to function relatively well. We'll break this section into the following:

1. The digestive system
2. Liver and kidneys
3. Metabolism
4. The immune system
5. The cardiovascular system
6. The brain
7. Bones, joints, and muscles
8. Skin and hair

After that, I will also briefly discuss medication, supplements, and the benefits of rest and sleep.

The whole idea in this section is not to bombard you with a lot of information, but help you take the initiative toward better healthcare. As you go, you will refine the methods in such a way that works best for you. Each person is different, and our activities are different as well.

## Your Digestive System

When we eat food, our body turns that food into energy by taking all the necessary vitamins, minerals, fiber, and carbohydrates from it. Once done, the body generates fecal material to be eliminated. It's a complex process that involves several steps. But I won't go into all the details; we will just focus on the major parts of the digestive process:

➢ The stomach
➢ The small intestine
➢ The pancreas, liver, and gallbladder
➢ The large intestine

- **The Stomach**

  Six things to note about the stomach:

  ➢ This is where the digestion starts, as a warm up
  ➢ It's an acidic area
  ➢ The ability of the stomach to produce adequate acid declines with age
  ➢ Cabbage juice might help you regulate the activities in your stomach. Licorice Root juice might help you release compound residue in your stomach.
  ➢ Aloe, as well, might help you refresh and smooth the activity of your stomach

- **The Small Intestine**

  The role of the small intestine is to absorb the minerals, vitamins, carbohydrates, protein and the different types of fat. The job of the intestine is to let the right nutrients flow into your blood stream meanwhile blocking the wrong elements from it. Keep in mind also that the main concern for the small intestine is to prevent bacteria overgrowth, which causes the following:

  ➢ Vitamin deficiency
  ➢ Bowel disease and improper functioning
  ➢ Autoimmune disorders
  ➢ Colon and breast cancer
  ➢ Skin conditions
  ➢ Fatigue
  ➢ Abdominal pain

  We tune up our small intestine by doing the following:

  ➢ Eating plenty of fiber
  ➢ Drinking fresh vegetable juice daily (I highly recommend you buy a juicer to mix your "greens.")

> ➤ Taking antioxidants to repair or prevent damage to intestinal cells caused by free radicals
> ➤ Taking flaxseed oil to lubricate and protect your intestinal lining.

• **The Pancreas**

The pancreas produces a digestive juice packed with enzymes needed to digest each of the main nutrients, which are sugar starches, proteins, and fats.

We tune up our pancreas by eating the following:

> ➤ Pineapple
> ➤ Papaya

• **The Liver**

The liver produces a fluid called bile. Bile is crucial in the absorption of fat and fatty acids, oils, and fat soluble vitamins. Bile also breaks down large sums of fat into smaller pieces. Bile keeps the intestines free from microorganisms, makes our feces soft, and smoothes the process of digestion and elimination of food.

• **The Gallbladder**

The gallbladder's job is to store bile until it is needed in the digestion and elimination process. A good way to cleanse both your liver and your gallbladder is to take some artichoke extract.

• **The Large Intestine**

The large intestine is also known as the colon, and it's much larger than the small intestine. All the nutrients from the food have been absorbed before going into the large intestine. However, the large intestine absorbs water, salt, and other elements.

A good way to cleanse your large intestine is to consume a lot of fiber, drink a lot of water, and eat an apple a day. Pears are also an excellent source of soluble fiber.

## Your Liver and Kidneys

- **The Liver**

Your liver is probably one of the most important organs in your body. It performs over 500 duties for the proper functioning of the human body.

Picture a clothes dryer. What happens if your filter gets clogged? Your clothes won't dry, which defeats the entire purpose of the dryer. This is a good analogy for the liver.

The main job of the liver is to accumulate all the waste and toxins of your body. Once it compiles all of it, then it rejects it from the body. If the liver, like a dryer, is not "cleaned," its purpose is defeated because it cannot do its job, which is to amass waste so that the body functions properly.

Three recommendations to cleanse your liver:

➢ Garlic
➢ Onion
➢ Silymarin (Milk thistle), which is a very powerful herb

- **The Kidneys**

The main job of the kidneys is to filter the blood and extract waste product and excess water and eliminate them from your body through urine.

To tune up your kidneys, drink at least 1.5 liters of water per day. Remember your body is at least 60% water, therefore drinking spring water or water filtered by reverse osmosis is crucial in the cleanup of your kidneys.

## Your Metabolism

Your metabolism is all the chemical processes that occur in your body and the amount of energy (calories) your body burns to maintain itself. Chemical processes include your food's digestion, the activity of your immune system, and the development of the body's organs.

Each one of us has a different rate at which our body processes chemical reactions. That's why it's so important to know your metabolic rate. Metabolism must function well because when metabolism functions properly, you are able to use your energy supply more efficiently, control your weight, and feel better and more energetic. It's important to check your metabolism if you are trying to maintain a healthy weight or to lose weight.

- **What is Your BMR?**

Basal metabolic rate (BMR) is the rate at which chemical processes in your body use energy when you are awake and not doing anything.

- **To Calculate Your BMR:**

➢ Men:

Divide your weight in pounds by 2.2. For example, if a man weighs 160 pounds, his BMR is 72, which means he burns 72 calories per hour without doing anything. If we multiply his BMR by 24 (for the hours in the day), we can conclude that this man needs a minimum of 1745 calories per day.

➢ Women:

Convert your weight to kilograms and multiply by 0.9. For example, if a woman weighs 160 pounds (72.5 kg), her BMR is 65 (72.5 x0.9), which means she burns 65 calories per hour without doing anything. If we multiply her BMR by 24, we can conclude that this woman needs a minimum of 1566 calories per day.

Keep in mind, the older we get, the slower our metabolism, and therefore, the easier to gain weight.

- **To boost metabolism:**

  ➢ Exercise more frequently
  ➢ Eat more vegetable, fruits, and legumes
  ➢ Drink natural herbal thermogenics tea (use with caution)
  ➢ Red Cayenne Peppers (use with caution)
  ➢ Reduce caffeine, alcohol, and sugar intake

## Your Immune System

Your immune system is your defense mechanism that protects the billions of cells in your body against outside intruders, such as viruses. Without a strong immune system, ordinary infections can lead to serious, life-threatening diseases. If your immune system is weak, the chances of getting an infection increases and the odds of having cancerous cells increases as well.

Let's say your immune system is an army defending your body against intruders. What is the army composed of? Who are the subordinates and generals in your army?

➢ Your Skin: Well-nourished and moist skin protects you against infections. Skin that is dry and cracked creates openings for infections.

➢ The Mucous Membrane: produces a fluid that tracks down microbes and prevents them from damaging the cells in your body. The mucus membrane is found in different organs of your body such as your lungs, genitals, and your digestive track.

➢ Specialized Cells: Throughout your body, you have specialized cells that are trained to recognize and destroy invaders, especially white blood cells. Your body produces about 12 million white blood cells every minute to fight off intruders.

- **To boost your immune system:**

  - ➤ Eat food rich with antioxidants
  - ➤ Beta carotene
  - ➤ Vitamin A, B1, B6, B12, C and E
  - ➤ Selenium
  - ➤ Zinc
  - ➤ Deep breathing
  - ➤ Exercise
  - ➤ Herbal: Echinacea
  - ➤ Herbal: Thymus extracts
  - ➤ Reduce alcohol, sweets and eliminate cigarettes
  - ➤ Promote stress-free environment

### Your Cardiovascular System

What an interesting organ the heart is! The heart is a very complex organ that works every single second of our lives. Therefore this is the organ we cannot afford to "mess with."

- **A brief overview of the heart**
  - ➤ The heart beats somewhere between 60-100 times a minute, approximately 100,000 times a day.
  - ➤ The heart pumps 5000 gallons of fluid a day.
  - ➤ During an average lifetime, the heart beats 2.5 billion times and pumps 100 trillion gallons of blood.
  - ➤ The heart pumps blood to 60,000 miles of blood vessel.
  - ➤ The heart does the most physical work of any muscle during a lifetime.

As we can see, the heart is by far the most important muscle or organ in the body. That is why we need to guard it, protect it, nurture it, and take special care of it.

Did you know that 7,000 people die annually in the United States due to murder? Staggering, isn't it? Now, consider this—250,000 people die every year from heart disease in this country. Two-hundred and fifty-thousand. That's 243,000 more people at risk of death by heart disease than murder.

Does this mean that the heart is dangerous or do our poor choices create dangerous physical conditions?

Let's do an overview of the most common problems and how to solve them:

> Atherosclerosis: the buildup of waxy materials called plaques (cholesterol, fatty acid, triglycerides) along the walls of the blood vessels.
> Thrombosis: formation of blood clots, which slows the blood flow.
> Heart attack: caused when the flow of blood is blocked to the heart.
> Stroke: occurs when an artery feeding the brain bursts.
> High Blood Pressure: The heart makes too much effort to pump blood through your body.
> Congestive Heart Failure (CHF): caused by the inability of the heart to effectively pump enough blood. This is due to long-term effects of high blood pressure, previous heart attack, and/or lung disease.
> Anemia: refers to blood abnormalities, e.g., not enough red cells, defective cells, or iron deficiencies.

The solutions to improve your cardiovascular system are simple: change your nutrition and your lifestyle.

• **For better nutrition, greatly reduce or eliminate the following**:
> Red meat
> Junk food
> Butter
> Fried foods
> Sweets (ice cream, pies, cookies)

- ➢ Salty foods
- ➢ Coffee and sodas
- ➢ Flour
- ➢ Margarine and hydrogenated oils

- **Substitute with:**
  - ➢ Fish rich in Omega 3 (such as salmon and mackerel)
  - ➢ Flaxseed oil
  - ➢ Increase intake of beans
  - ➢ White poultry
  - ➢ Soy products
  - ➢ Wheat
  - ➢ Fruit, vegetable, legumes
  - ➢ Herbal teas
  - ➢ Water
  - ➢ Olive oil
  - ➢ Fiber
  - ➢ Nuts (specifically walnuts)
  - ➢ Garlic
  - ➢ Turmeric
  - ➢ Celery
  - ➢ COQ10
  - ➢ Extract of hawthorn berries
  - ➢ Vitamin C, B6 & Calcium

- **Add to that a lifestyle change**
  - ➢ Exercise at least 4 times a week for a minimum of 30 minutes
  - ➢ Avoid smoking and other type of inhalants
  - ➢ Always eat a good breakfast
  - ➢ Stay away from negative people
  - ➢ Develop loving relationships
  - ➢ Stop complaining and become a grateful person
  - ➢ Sleep at least 7 to 8 hours a day

> Stop being pessimistic, instead become optimistic about your own future. Encourage other people, and let the words coming out of your month be:
> - Encouraging
> - Hopeful
> - Joyful
> - Full of love and compassion

## Your Brain

The brain is like the executive power of the body. This is where all the commands come from.

- **Did you know that**:
  > the brain accounts for 2% of your body weightthe brain consumes 20% of your body's energy and oxygenat birth, the brain contains 10 billion neuronsyour brain has an estimated 100 trillion connections
  > every day, about 50 thousand brain cells die

- **Duties of the brain include**:
  > regulating breathing, blood pressure …controlling speech
  > helping with creativity
  > decision making
  > mathematical calculations
  > storing memories
  > and much more

In order to improve the functions of your brain, you have to take into consideration that your brain is mostly made of fats. In fact, we need to nourish our brain with the right essential fatty acid in order for it to function properly.

- **To improve your brain functions**:
  > Take Omega 3 fatty acid

> Reduce stress
> Reduce alcohol
> Increase potassium and magnesium while reducing sodium intake
> Take Vitamins B1, B2, B3, B5, B6 and B12 (You can do this with a multi-complex vitamin)
> Take antioxidants
> Increase choline. Choline can be found in peanuts, soy foods, Brussels sprouts, oatmeal, cabbage, cauliflower, spinach, lettuce, and potatoes
> Blueberries
> Flavonoid- rich foods such as bilberry, grape seed, pine bark, or ginkgo biloba
> Do some brain exercises. Solve problems, solve crossword puzzles, etc.

The reception of the five senses comes from the brain ...

- **To improve the brain's reception of the five senses**:
  > For taste: increase your Zinc level. While we are in the subject of taste, it's important to remind you to brush your teeth *at least* twice a day. More importantly, to floss your teeth at least five times a week. Some studies suggest that flossing your teeth may protect us from heart diseases.
  > For smell: increase your Zinc level.
  > For touch: focus and pay more attention to what you are touching.
  > For hearing: increase your zinc and Vitamin B12; Once a month, use a wax-removing kit containing a soft rubber syringe to flush your ears. (This helps a lot.)
  > For vision: increase Vitamin A, C, and E; increase flavonoid-rich extract foods such as bilberry, grape seed, pine bark, or ginkgo biloba; eat corn, kiwi, red grapes, squash, bell peppers, greens (such as spinach, kale, chard, etc.), cucumbers, peas,

honeydew, celery, Brussels sprouts, scallions, green beans, oranges, broccoli, apples, mangos, peaches, tomato paste/juice.

## Your Bones

Your bones are living organs that require nurture and care. You have about 200 bones in your body and each week you recycle 7% of your bone mass.

- **Bones play the following roles:**
  - ➢ Your bones support your body and protect the soft organs.
  - ➢ Your bones are a reservoir for future use of the following: minerals, calcium. phosphorus, magnesium, and manganese.
  - ➢ Bone tissues are where blood cells are born.

- **To improve your bone structure:**
  - ➢ Consume a healthy diet (more greens, less processed foods, low sugar intake).
  - ➢ Consume adequate amount of protein.
  - ➢ Increase consumption of soy foods.
  - ➢ Dramatically reduce alcohol, caffeine, and soda intake.
  - ➢ Increase calcium intake by:
    - • Plant foods such as tofu, kale, spinach, and turnip greens.
    - • Calcium supplements with a combination of calcium carbonate and calcium citrate.

## Your Joints

Your joints are where your bones meet. Joints have a dual function, they hold your skeleton together and give mobility. Most of the joints in the body are separated by a fluid filled membrane.

- **Joints are located all over the body, including:**
  - ➢ Shoulders
  - ➢ Elbows

> ➤ Fingers
> ➤ Hips
> ➤ Knees
> ➤ Toes
> ➤ Between the ribs
> ➤ And much more

What we really need to understand about our joints is that they are mainly made by cartilage, which is resilient and flexible. But, like every other part of your body, your cartilage needs some nourishment and nutrition otherwise you may be subject to diseases such as osteoarthritis, a condition resulting from loss of cartilage.

- **To improve your joints:**
  > ➤ Exercise and stretch
  > ➤ Diet rich in plant foods
  > ➤ Antioxidants
  > ➤ Increase intake of Omega 3 fatty acid
  > ➤ Flaxseed oil
  > ➤ Maintain appropriate weight
  > ➤ Take Vitamin C (greatly helps cartilage)
  > ➤ Vitamin A, B6, E, Zinc, and Copper
  > ➤ If necessary, physical therapy with periodic ice, massage, rest, and acupuncture
  > ➤ Glucosamine Sulfate (By itself; not combined with anything else)
  > ➤ Ginger
  > ➤ Phytodolor
  > ➤ Bosewellia seratta
  > ➤ Curcumin
  > ➤ Cream containing capsicum (found in cayenne pepper)
  > ➤ MSM (consult your physician)
  > ➤ Devils Claw (good for back pain)
  > ➤ White Willow bark

➢ Cherries

➢ Blueberries

## Your Muscles

Whenever I think about muscles, I think about the gym and weight lifting. It's amazing when you go to the gym and see some people lifting weights like crazy, looking at themselves in the mirror and walking around confident, strong and, maybe sometimes, arrogant. I wonder how many times the gym-addicted individual walks around thinking, "You mess with me and I will kick your butt," or something like that.

Let me tell you my story. I used to hate the gym and my rationale was simple: it's too addictive. Once you start lifting weights, you soon want to lift heavier weights because your body becomes accustomed to where you began or where you left off. Before you know it, you start by spending an hour, then an hour and a half, then after that, two hours, then two and a half hours. Soon, you could find yourself spending half a day in the gym. Weight-lifting is time-consuming and addictive. Then, if you spend a week or two not exercising, it's extremely hard on your muscles when you start back.

Then I decided, "Forget about it; I am not going back to the gym". Instead I decided to go to the park and run for an hour, once or twice a week. But let me tell you what happened. Running on the hard surface *pounded* on my knees. So much pressure is applied to your joints when you run, for some, the damage can go beyond the point of repair. And I think that's what happened to me, I messed up my left knee joint. I don't know if my knee is messed up for life, but I can no longer run, play basketball, or play soccer on hard surface.

So I joined the gym again and I now firmly believe that *everyone* should have a gym membership. There are so many reasons why you should join a gym, a few of which are:

- **Your Health**

  The more I read health books, the more I put what I read into practice. I have become totally convinced that exercise is a requirement for good physical and mental health. Remember, exercise stimulates your metabolism, helps with digesting, improves sleep, boosts your immune system, helps with your cardiovascular system, etc.

- **The Equipment**

  Take my situation, for example. I have a knee joint problem and a back problem that keep me from performing certain exercises. But the wide variety of equipment at the gym provides me with plenty of alternatives. I use the elliptical and Stairmaster machine for cardio as substitute for running. The gym I attend has a basketball court with a special wood floor which reduces the amount of pressure on my knees when I play basketball.

  Many gyms even have a pool which is good for the back, and also several machines to help strengthen the core muscles, which is also good for the back.

- **The Flexibility**

  The gym is especially good for the following two reasons:
  - Hours

  Many gyms are open from 5 a.m. to midnight, or even 24 hours a day, allowing for anyone—no matter how busy—to fit exercise into their busy schedule.
  - The weather

  If you have a fitness program or you decide for the next year to seriously improve your exercise activities, by joining a gym, the weather becomes irrelevant. You can exercise despite the weather.

- **The People**

  In my opinion, most people go the gym for health reasons. Not only can you see and meet people who will inspire you to get into a better physical shape, but it's also an incredible place to hear the testimonies of others as well.

Check this out: remember, I have a back problem and, quite honestly, it's one of those health challenges that no matter the physical position I am in, my back hurts. One Sunday afternoon I went to the pool at the gym and while I was coming out of the pool I saw this other gentleman getting ready to leave as well. While he was putting his shirt back on, I saw that he had some surgical scars on his lower back. I asked him if he had a lower back problem, and indeed he did. For the next thirty minutes, I learned that this man, age 57, had back problems since he was 30. He'd had surgery at 52. Over the years, he had gained much experience and wisdom, all of which he shared with me. He showed me some key exercises to practice every day that would help improve my back. He also shared with me how he felt before and after surgery. What had taken this man 20 years to learn, he was able to share with me in half hour, information I would not have learned had I not been at the gym.

- **The Classes**

  Lastly, I have to mention the classes offered at the gym. There are all sorts of classes, from swimming lessons, yoga, bicycle, aerobics, Zumba, Pilates, etc. Depending on your membership, sometimes those classes are at no extra cost. It's totally worth it.

CAUTION: CONSULT YOUR PHYSICIAN BEFORE
STARTING ANY EXERCISE PROGRAM. BE VERY
CAREFUL NOT TO GET INJURED IN THE GYM.
DON'T OVERDO IT.

Let's now go back to your muscles.

- **Your body has 3 types of muscles:**
  - ➤ Skeletal muscles: located around your bones
  - ➤ Muscles of your internal organs

➤ Cardiac muscles

The key thing to remember about your muscles is that they are elastic—like a rubber band—and if you stretch too hard, the muscle will burst out and break.

- **To improve your muscles:**
  ➤ If you are going to lift weights, make sure you warm up first and then stretch afterward.
  ➤ Make sure your diet includes adequate antioxidants to reduce muscle soreness.
  ➤ Take a Vitamin B complex, vitamins C and E.
  ➤ Engage in weight-lifting exercises for at least 20 minutes, 3 times a week
  ➤ Eat flavonoid-rich foods such as cherries, berries, and citrus fruit.
  ➤ Increase flaxseed oil intake.

### Your Skin

The skin is a protective layer that guards you from things such as bacteria, injury, extreme temperatures, pollutants, toxic wastes, etc. When you think about the skin, think of it as a protective layer or an effective shield. Your skin is a reflection of your overall health.

- **Your skin also helps with:**
  ➤ Your immune system.
  ➤ The production of Vitamin D for your bones.
  ➤ Detoxification of your body.
  ➤ Destruction of cancer-causing chemicals before they harm your cells.

- **We improve our skin by:**
  ➤ Eating the highest quality nutrition.
  ➤ Not using harsh chemicals, for example certain body soaps.

> ➢ Spending time in the light or outdoors for a tan, but not more than 15 minutes, otherwise you can burn your skin. Depending on your skin type, you might even want to use a sunscreen to be on the safe side.
> ➢ Getting a natural colon cleansing, this helps both digestion and skin.
> ➢ Increasing fiber intake.
> ➢ Increasing antioxidant levels and Vitamin A, C, and E.
> ➢ Taking Omega 3.
> ➢ Dramatically increasing your water consumption.
> ➢ Seriously decreasing junk food, fatty foods, and foods loaded with sugar.

### Hair

It's interesting to note that men and woman alike have millions of hair scattered over their body. Human hair serves a number of purposes, such as (on the head) to protect the scalp from the sun's rays; to keep foreign matter out of the body (via the eyes, the nose, and the ears). Hairs on our body regulate body temperature and function as receptors on the skin that help us experience the sense of touch. But most of us think only about how our hair *looks*. So how do we keep our hair growing and avoid hair loss, while maintaining its shine and tone?

- **To avoid hair loss and maintain shine and tone:**
  - ➢ Don't spend too much time in the sun.
  - ➢ Reduce intake of certain types of drugs.
  - ➢ Intake of Vitamin A, B6, C, E, and Zinc.
  - ➢ Intake of fiber.
  - ➢ Intake of complex carbohydrates.
  - ➢ Intake of palmetto berry extract
  - ➢ Increase antioxidant levels
  - ➢ Intake flaxseed oil

➢ Herbs such as rosemary, ginseng, and lavender helps

➢ Drink plenty of water

### Medications

I am not at all against medication. I see medication as a temporary relief. But, in my opinion, medication doesn't solve your problems; it only fixes your problem temporarily. I believe changing lifestyle, better nutrition, exercise, and taking supplements is a better *cure*.

### 5. Supplements

There are lots of different opinions out there about supplements. Some people think buying supplements is a waste of time and money. I believe supplements are crucial and a must if you want to live well. You will have to choose which one of these opinions seems right for you.

Here are the reasons why I believe supplements are important:

➢ The source of our foods: from the get go you have a problem because the soil used to grow crops is impoverished. This means that the crops themselves are insufficient in terms of minerals and vitamin. That's why organic crops are better.

➢ Transit and shelf time of our food: There is a big time delay between when the crops are picked and your consumption. That time delay and the preservatives added to maintain the freshness of the food reduces its quality and effectiveness.

➢ Toxins and chemicals: Our busy life creates a lot of stress to the body: work, family, community, and social interactions accumulate the stress level in our body. Taking supplements helps alleviate a lot of this and supports your body by providing the nutrition needed to function optimally.

### 6. Rest

I emphasize the importance of rest later on in the book. But I do have to say that there are a lot of theories about why sleeping is so important. But here are some unquestionable and indisputable truths about sleeping:

> We all do it.
> Without enough sleep, we feel tired during our regular activities.
> It relaxes and refreshes us.
> Finally, in the Bible specifically in the Old Testament, we learn that God rested after creating the world. If God found it necessary, why not us?

# CHAPTER 5

# NUTRITION

In the first book of the Bible, Genesis, we find the following scriptures: "For dust you are and to dust you will return" (Genesis 3:19 NIV). A lot is found within these few words.

All of us, without exception, will physically die. Our physical bodies are finite. However, if you want the full number of years you have been given to be *good* and *healthy* years, you must take care of your body. Better care can often mean greater longevity.

Now let's say you have a T-shirt with a hole in it that you intend to stitch. Will you use a piece of metal for the thread or thread made of cotton? Or, let's say you are trying to grow an apple tree. Will you nourish the sapling with soda and French fries or with good soil and water?

Taking care of our bodies does not have to be complicated. For example, did you know that if you take pure lemon juice concentrate, you are helping your immune system fight bacteria and viruses? Or that by eating pineapple, you not only help with inflammation associated with arthritis and join paint, but you are also aiding your digestive system.

Did you know that carrots are the richest fruit in carotene, which helps your eyes and lungs? Or that when you eat blueberries— the richest food in antioxidant compounds—it can help clean your cells, which aids in the prevention of cancer, heart disease, and memory loss.

How is it that specific fruits and vegetables contain specific properties that heal and protect specific parts of your body? Why does the lemon provide enough Vitamin C to boost the immune system and not enough antioxidants to prevent cancer? I wish I knew the answer. But surely God has provided us with more than enough of what we need to take care of the body He has given to us.

Is it possible that the ground or the soil produces almost everything our body needs in order to function properly, effectively, and vigorously? Yes. All plants, fruits, salads, nuts, seeds, beans and legumes, grains, herbs, spices, and vegetables come from the ground, and all of them, to some degree, contain properties that can help you:

➢ Heal
➢ Energize
➢ Cleanse
➢ Prolong life
➢ Much more

I have read several health books, watched a lot of nutritional videos and attended numerous seminars and classes. In my opinion, what they all have in common is this: When it comes to nutrition, the more processed your food is, the greater your chances are of getting sick and staying sick. And, in your nutrition supplementation, the more modifications there are between the ground and your mouth, the less nutritional benefit you will receive and the greater your chances of developing unnecessary disease.

## So what's the problem?

The problem boils down to this:

- **Poor choices**

Sometimes we make poor choices due to lack of knowledge. I remember a few years back before I knew much about nutrition, my belly was a little flabby, and I wanted to have a "six-pack." I started to do some sit ups every morning. For nutrition, I remembered the advertisement from Subway "Eat Fresh," and so I went there almost every day. After about two weeks I realized that my belly was not forming the six-pack. I got discouraged and stopped doing my sit ups. Later, I learned that the flour in the sandwich's bread directly converts into sugar, which was one of the biggest things preventing me from having the core I wanted.

- **Taste**

A lot of times, processed food tastes better than natural foods. We are all guilty—I know I am—of preferring ice cream over watermelon or oatmeal cookies over an apple. But if we want to live healthy lives, we have to make the right choices.

- **Easy access and convenience**

It's easier and more convenient to stop by a fast food restaurant to grab something to eat instead of buying groceries and cooking at home and walking around with a lunch bag.

> ➤ These same "problems" can be our "solutions" if we make educated and better food selection.
> ➤ Look for *nutritional* foods instead of *tasteful* food.
> ➤ Look for restaurants with healthy menu selections when we eat out.

In conclusion, the more natural and simple your food is, the better you will feel and perform.

Recently I took the "Apple Test." I strongly recommend it. You may be asking, "What is the Apple Test?"

There is an old saying that goes, "An apple a day keeps the doctor away." About two years ago, knowing all the benefits of an apple, I started eating an apple every day. Around once a week, I'd go to the grocery store and grab a bag of apples for the week. But one day, for some reason, I decided to buy a bag of organic apples. The price difference was probably $2. Let me tell you something … It was like eating a totally different fruit. The taste between the organic apple and the regular apple is significant. Try it.

But the difference doesn't stop with apples. There is a difference between everything organic and non-organic.

Imagine this: *day in and day out* you have been feeding your body with food that doesn't *properly nourish* you. The accumulation of that type of behavior is a disaster, prohibiting your body from proper nutrition.

## Nutrition Formula

Here is an interesting story I would like to share: In the building where I used to work, they always had a police car watching the building. One day, as I was leaving the office, I approached one of the officers on duty and told him that I had some of the best supplements to help him lose weight and at the same time increase his energy. Here was his answer:

"I don't take supplements. I don't eat salads or vegetables, and I believe the entire supplement industry is a scam."

I thought the officer was out of his mind. But then he said, "If I were to eat healthy every day, and one day I don't eat healthy, I will die because my body won't be able to adjust to the change."

Seeing that he was so narrow-minded, I simply replied, "Have a nice day." A few days later, I started to think about what the officer had said and I realized he had a point.

For instance, not all fats are bad for the body. Monounsaturated fat such as olive oil is *good* for your body. So, after talking with that officer, I realized *variety* is the key for good health, while improper balance is destructive to good health.

So I decided to follow the following principle: I will eat healthy six days a week and have one "cheat day," my junk food day.

Here is my formula for proper nutrition and a list I will recommend:

➢ 6 days of healthy eating (natural, whole foods) and 1 "cheat day."
➢ Make certain my calorie intake and output are in balance.
➢ Drink at least 1 liter of water every day.
➢ Eat as many organic fruits and vegetable as possible.

➤ Take daily supplements such as Vitamin B complex and Omega 3.

➤ Dramatically reduce or nearly eliminate soda intake, sugars, simple carbohydrates, smoking, and alcohol. (Remember that consuming large amounts of rapidly-digestible sugar and high-fructose corn syrup causes a spike in blood sugar and insulin, which can lead to inflammation and insulin resistance, both of which may increase your risk of stroke, heart disease, diabetes, obesity, and cancer.)

➤ Have a 15-minutes rule: If you finish a meal and are still hungry, wait 15 minutes before even thinking about getting anything else to eat.

➤ Take antioxidants daily. I love to drink hot tea, rich in antioxidant, in the mornings.

➤ Avoid eating fried foods and red meat as much as possible. (At a most basic level, fried foods are unhealthy because they tend to be very high in fat and calories. But, deep frying also robs food of nutrients. Excessive red meat leads to cholesterol-clogged arteries, which may lead to heart problems.)

➤ Drink a glass of water immediately before eating (not the other way around) for weight control.

Now I must confess that I don't follow this list to the letter every week. But I try my best to stay within range. I hope you will too.

# CHAPTER 6

# BEST FOODS

This chapter is a list of the best nutrition that you can put in your body for energy and vitality for short term and long term health goals. In writing this chapter, I had to go through several books to find out the best fruits, vegetables, beans, legumes, salads, and much more, in order to create an *easy to read, compact, straightforward, informative* list that highlights all the nutritional and health benefits of whole, plant-grown foods (unprocessed, unrefined foods that grew from the ground). I wrote that chapter in such a way that even a ten year old would be able to read and understand the content without having to go through a dictionary for not understanding technical language, jargon, or specialized vocabulary.

As you read this chapter, at some point you will surely realized that whole, plant-grown foods provide almost every single nutrient and property necessary for you to live a long and healthy life. Not only do whole, plant-grown foods provide you with the best nutrition, they also provide you with the best disease prevention known to mankind. Please read carefully and enjoy.

Here is an index listing by alphabetical order:

| **<u>Fruits</u>** | **<u>Vegetables</u>** |
|---|---|
| Apple | Asparagus |
| Apricot | Avocados |
| Bananas | Beets |
| Blueberries | Bell peppers |
| Cranberries | Broccoli |
| Figs | Brussels sprouts |
| Grape fruits | Cabbage |
| Grapes | Carrots |
| Lemons | Celery |
| Papaya | Garlic |
| Pears | Green beans |
| Plums | Green peas |
| Watermelon | Kale/Mustard |
| | Mushroom |
| | Onion |
| | Romaine lettuce |
| | Spinach |
| | Squash |
| | Sweet potatoes |
| | Tomatoes |

# Beans & Grain

Black beans
Brown rice
Kidney beans
Lentils
Navy beans
Oats
Quinoa
Soybeans
Whole wheat

# Herb and Spices

Basil
Cilantro
Cinnamon
Ginger
Mint
Oregano
Parsley
Rosemary
Sage
Thyme
Turmeric

# Seeds and Nuts

Almonds
Cashew
Coco beans
Flaxseeds
Peanuts
Pumpkin seeds
Sesame seeds
Sunflower seeds
Walnuts

# FRUITS

Fruits

# Apples

| CHARACTERISTICS | THE GOOD NEWS FOR YOU |
|---|---|

1)  Flavonoid Quercetin

- Anti-cancer properties.
- Anti-inflammatory properties.
- Helps maintain a healthy heart.
- Promotes lung health and helps with asthma.
- Helps prevent heart disease.

2)  Pectin/Soluble Fiber

- Helps lower bad cholesterol.
- Helps prevent colon cancer.
- Helps relieve constipation.
- Promotes digestive health.

3)  Antioxidants

- Rich in powerful antioxidants that help cleanse the cells in the body
- Highest level of antioxidant properties.

## Apricots

| CHARACTERISTICS | THE GOOD NEWS FOR YOU |
| --- | --- |

1) General Information

- Excellent source of vitamin A and vitamin C.
- Contains antioxidants to protect against free radicals.
- Important to maintain healthy eye functions, reduce the risk of cataracts.
- Great source of potassium.

2) Beta-Carotene/ Beta-Cryptoxanthin

- A powerful antioxidant that protects the body from cancer caused by free radicals.
- Contains anti-aging properties.
- Promotes vision health.

3) Weight Control

- Great source of fiber that assists digestion and helps with weight loss.

- A fat-free food and a fantastic snack alternative.

4) Tryptophan

- Improves sleep patterns and promotes better sleep.
- Regulates appetite and overall mood.
- Can help with depression and anxiety.

# Bananas

| CHARACTERISTICS | THE GOOD NEWS FOR YOU |
| --- | --- |

1) General Information

- Excellent source of potassium, which helps maintain normal blood pressure.
- Bananas contain vitamin B6, which helps maintain the cardiovascular system.
- Contains high amounts of fiber.
- Promotes overall stomach health and protects the stomach against ulcers.

2) Potassium

- Essential for maintaining normal blood pressure and heart functions.
- Helps the body's muscles and nerves function properly.
- May increase energy level.
- May help in maintaining the density and strength of bones.

3) Dietary Fiber

- Promotes digestive health; may help relieve constipation.
- Helps normalize movement in the digestive tract.
- Helps maintain normal cholesterol level.

# Blueberries

| CHARACTERISTICS | THE GOOD NEWS FOR YOU |
|---|---|

1) General Information

- Blueberries contain the most antioxidants of all fruits.
- High in vitamin C to boost immune system.
- A powerhouse in terms of nutrients, a must for optimal health.
- Great source of dietary fiber, which promotes digestion.
- Resveratrol levels in blueberries help maintain a healthy heart.
- Helps destroy urinary tract infections.

2) Pterostillbene

- Highly effective in lowering cholesterol levels.
- May help prevent cancer in general.
- Helps prevent diabetes by stabilizing blood sugar and insulin levels.

3) Anthocyanins

- Increases overall health of heart by helping lower cholesterol levels and blood pressure.
- Protects the collagen that holds the heart muscle together.
- Improves memory and fights against memory loss due to aging.

# Cranberries

## CHARACTERISTICS

## THE GOOD NEWS FOR YOU

1) General Information

- Excellent source of vitamin C.
- Helps prevent urinary tract infections.
- Great source of fiber for the digestive system.
- Decreases level of bad cholesterol.
- Incredible source of antioxidants.
- May prevent heart disease.

2) Quinic Acid

- Prevents calcium stones from forming by acidifying the urine.
- Can be used to help treat kidney stones by breaking up the calcium that forms them.

3) Proanthocyanidin

- Excellent for overall health of the urinary track.

- Prevents urinary tract infections by making it difficult for bacteria to grow.
- Protects stomach lining against ulcers caused by bacteria attaching to stomach lining.

# Figs

CHARACTERISTICS

THE GOOD NEWS FOR YOU

1) General Information

- Excellent source of fiber for the digestive system.
- May protect against heart disease.
- High in potassium, which regulates blood pressure and prevents hypertension.
- Great source of natural energy.
- Fig leaves contain anti-diabetic properties, reducing the amount of insulin needed by diabetics.

2) Phytosterols

- Lowers cholesterol levels by blocking its absorption in the body.
- Reduces risk of heart disease by preventing arteries from clogging.

3) Potassium

- Great source of potassium.

- Helps lower the risk of high blood pressure.
- Helps muscles and nerves work properly.
- Helps maintain the density and strength of bones due to its ability to retain calcium.

## Grapefruit

CHARACTERISTICS          THE GOOD NEWS FOR YOU

1)  General Information

- Excellent source of vitamin C, which is good for the immune system.
- High in antioxidants, which can help prevent cancers and prostate problems.
- Great source of dietary fiber.
- Helps regulate blood pressure.
- Helps lower bad cholesterol (LDL).
- Helps the body to promote cellular energy.

2)  Limonoids

- Helps produce glutathione -S-transferase which helps the body flush toxins.
- Fights against cancers that affect the stomach, mouth, colon, and lungs.

3) Naringenin

- Helps lower cholesterol.
- Naringenin reduces the risk of developing prostate (an important gland in the male reproductive system) cancer.
- Helps repair DNA.

# Grapes

| CHARACTERISTICS | THE GOOD NEWS FOR YOU |
|---|---|

1) General Information

- Excellent source of manganese, which helps in cellular absorption.
- High in vitamin C, which lowers the risk of cancer.
- Improves overall heart health.

2) Flavonoid

- Helps regulate cholesterol levels.
- Protects the heart from arteriosclerosis (hardening of the arties) and improves blood circulation.

3) Resveratrol

- Prevents various forms of cancer, and heart disease.
- Keeps the heart strong by preventing blood vessels from contracting.
- Helps fight off viral infections.
- Prevents generative nerve disease.
- Inhibits viral infections.

4)  Quercetin

- Improves healthy cholesterol levels (HDL).
- Quercetin has an anti-clotting effect important in preventing blood clots.

# Lemons

CHARACTERISTICS

THE GOOD NEWS FOR YOU

1)  General Information

- Excellent and high source of vitamin C, which helps neutralize free radicals that can damage blood vessels.
- Boosts the immune system.
- Contains unique flavonoid phytonutrients that are shown to give protection from cardiovascular disease.
- A must for the overall health of the immune system, promotes overall optimal health.
- Helpful in the kitchen because it is useful to marinate meat and fish, and adds flavor to side dishes.

- Lemon may also promote respiratory health due to its antioxidant ability.

2) Limonene

- Shown to help prevent against breast cancer.
- Lowers bad cholesterol levels.

3) Rutin

- Promotes stronger and healthier veins.
- Neutralizes free radicals that can damage cell structure.

# Papaya

CHARACTERISTICS

THE GOOD NEWS FOR YOU

1) General Information

- High in vitamin C, which boosts the immune system to help prevent infections.
- High in vitamin A, which comes from the beta-carotene and beta-cryptoxanthin. Protects eyes from free radicals caused by pollution, smoking, or radiation.
- High in potassium, which helps to decrease chances of developing a stroke and improve blood pressure control.

2) Papain/Chymopapain

- Helps the digestive system in breaking down protein.

- Lowers inflammation throughout the body helping   those with arthritis, asthma,  or eczema.

3)   Folate

- Good source of folate, which is important for pregnant women and essential in the  growth of a healthy fetus. It  is known to prevent cardiovascular disease and poor nerve function in  infants.

# Pears

CHARACTERISTICS

THE GOOD NEWS FOR YOU

1) General Information

- Great source of fiber which is important for preventing colon cancer.
- Contains Phytosterols, which promote overall heart health.
- Good source of vitamin C, which helps to protect damaged cells.
- Contain high antioxidant levels.
- Prevents constipation and ensures regularity.

2) Hydroxycinnamic

- Anti-cancer properties because of its ability to prevent oxidation in cells.
- Natural anti-bacterial that fights off unwanted bacteria in the body.

- Prevents gastroenteritis, which causes inflammation in the stomach.

3)  Phytosterols

- Helps lower cholesterol levels.
- Improves overall blood circulation.
- Greatly reduces the production and absorption of bad cholesterol.

# Plums

CHARACTERISTICS     THE GOOD NEWS FOR YOU

1)  General Information

- Rich source of antioxidants
- Fantastic source of vitamin C to help the overall cells in the body.
- Contains anthocyanins that protect against heart disease.
- Good source of fiber for digestive system.

2)  Phenolic Compounds

- Beneficial to maintain healthy brain function.
- Effective in fighting against free radicals.
- Protects healthy fats circulating throughout our bloodstream.

3) Catechins

- Protects bad cholesterol from oxidizing, which can lead to heart problems.
- Powerful antioxidants that help keep the body at its optimal status.

# Watermelon

CHARACTERISTICS          THE GOOD NEWS FOR YOU

1) General Information

- Great source of vitamin C, which can protect against cardiovascular disease.
- High in vitamin A, which protects the skin and is also used to help treat acne.
- Good source of potassium and magnesium, which helps keep blood pressure levels stable.
- Contains anti-aging properties.

2) Lycopene

- Powerful antioxidant.
- Important for cardiovascular health, can help prevent stroke and heart attack.
- Helps protect against prostate cancer.
- Helps protect skin from sun damage.

3) Arginine

- Improves blood flow in the cardiovascular system.
- Removes excess sugar from bloodstream.
- Helps regulate weight.

# VEGETABLES

# Asparagus

CHARACTERISTICS        THE GOOD NEWS FOR YOU

1)  General Information

- Good source of essential vitamins A and C, which are powerful antioxidants for cellular health.
- Contains a large combination of B vitamins, important for maintaining healthy blood sugar levels, heart health, and cellular division.
- Promotes overall digestive health.
- Has been used to treat problems involving swelling, such as arthritis and rheumatism.
- Promotes overall energy production.

2)  Vitamin K

- Bone building ingredient, which promotes overall bone health.
- Helps maintain proper blood mass level.

3) Insulin

- Good source of calcium and magnesium.

- Helps digestion by stimulating the growth of healthy bacteria in the gut.
- The insulin feeds bacteria that are linked to lower risks of developing colon cancer and allergies.

# Avocados

| CHARACTERISTICS | THE GOOD NEWS FOR YOU |
|---|---|

1) General Information

- Contains a good amount of vitamin K, essential for keeping blood thickness healthy and maintaining a healthy bone structure.
- Good source of potassium, which helps prevent circulatory diseases such as high blood pressure or stroke.
- Promotes overall heart health.
- Good source of antioxidants that protect cells from free radical oxidative damage.

2) Oleic Acid

- Oleic acid is a healthy fat that promotes heart health.
- Shown to lower bad cholesterol and raise healthy cholesterol levels.
- Lowers the risk of developing breast cancer.

3) Vitamin E

- Boosts the immune system.
- Important to keep skin healthy and bright.
- Prevents various forms of heart disease.
- Allows cells to communicate effectively.
- Protects skin from ultraviolet light.

# Beets

CHARACTERISTICS        THE GOOD NEWS FOR YOU

1)  General Information

- Provides more antioxidants than onion, celery, spinach, broccoli and carrots.
- Contains a high amount of folate, which is important for cellular production.
- Fiber content is special in beets and is linked to lower cases of colon cancer.
- Beets contain high levels of vitamins A & C, which are two powerful antioxidants.

2)  Betalains

- Powerful antioxidant shown to protect the liver from free radicals.

97

- Betalains helps cells to detoxify themselves from harmful substances.
- Shown to lower high blood pressure.
- Prevents the beginnings of cancerous activity.

3) Manganese

- Helps the body maintain healthy blood sugar levels.
- Essential for strong and healthy bones.
- Antioxidant that protects cells from free radical damage.

# Bell peppers

CHARACTERISTICS    THE GOOD NEWS FOR YOU

1) General Information

- Excellent levels of vitamin C, which provides protection from free radicals.
- Great source of vitamin A, which is good for overall vision health.
- Protection against the development of lung cancer.
- Good source of dietary fiber, which can help lower cholesterol.
- Ability to effectively neutralize free radicals throughout the body.
- Good source of vitamin B6, which has been shown to decrease risk of heart diseases, stroke, Alzheimer's disease and osteoporosis.

2) Lycopene

- Important for cardiovascular health by blocking bad cholesterol from clogging arteries.
- Shown to be beneficial to the prostate gland, lowering the risk of developing prostate cancer.
- May help promote optimal cellular health.

# Broccoli

CHARACTERISTICS                THE GOOD NEWS FOR YOU

1) General Information

- One of the most nutritious vegetables.
- Contains high level of vitamins A, C, and K, all of which are essential in supporting general health.
- Rich in folic acid, which is a form of vitamin B, which is healthy for the heart.
- Provides a lot of protection against different types of cancer.
- Good source of dietary fiber, protein, and calcium.

2) Sulforaphane

- Boosts the effectiveness of detoxifying enzymes in the liver.
- Provides protection against tumor development.
- Connected to lower risks of breast and colon cancer.

3) Lutein/Zeaxanthin

- Protects against degenerative eye disease.
- Protects eyes from free radicals caused by pollution, smoking, or radiation.

# Brussels sprouts

| CHARACTERISTICS | THE GOOD NEWS FOR YOU |
|---|---|

1) General Information

- High levels of vitamins A and C, which help boost the immune system.
- Vitamin K, which keeps bones from easily fracturing.
- Folate content supports the production of red blood cells responsible for carrying oxygen throughout the body.
- High concentration of lutein and zeaxanthin protect the eyes.
- Great source of fiber, which promotes digestive health.

2) Glutathione

- Protects fatty tissues from free radicals, which can damage arteries and cause a heart attack.
- Helps detoxify the liver from harmful substances.

- Helps reduce inflammation, which is the root of many health conditions such as heart disease and cancer.

3) Omega 3 Fatty Acids

- Helps prevent cancer cell growth throughout the body.
- Gives support to anti-inflammatory messenger molecules, which help conditions such as arthritis.
- Promotes brain health and joint flexibility.

# Cabbage

## CHARACTERISTICS

### THE GOOD NEWS FOR YOU

1) General Information

- Good source of vitamin C, which boosts the immune system.
- Good source of vitamin K, which helps prevent age-related bone loss.
- Contains dietary fiber, which promotes colon health.
- Contains Sulforaphane, which assists the liver in detoxifying the body of harmful substances.
- Reduces risk of lung, stomach, and colon cancer.
- Cabbage juice is capable of healing ulcers.

2) Phytonutrients

- Activates body antioxidant and detoxification mechanisms.
- Provides protection against breast cancer.
- Improves the way estrogen is broken down in the liver.

3) Sulforaphane

- Boosts the effectiveness of detoxifying enzymes in the liver.
- Connected to lower risks of breast and colon cancer.
- Increases overall body detoxification capabilities.

# Carrots

CHARACTERISTICS | THE GOOD NEWS FOR YOU

1) General Information

- A major source of vitamin A, which promotes healthy lungs and eyes.
- Beta carotene helps promote vision health and boosts the immune system.
- Contains high amounts of vitamin K, which is important in the building of strong bones.
- Contains vitamin C, which helps the immune system stay strong.
- Protects against cardiovascular and heart diseases.

2) Carotenoids

- Powerful antioxidants.
- Protects cells from harmful free radicals.
- Linked to a reduced risk of developing heart disease.

3) Vitamin A

- Promotes lung health.
- Gives protection against certain cancers.
- Excellent for eye heath.
- May help against emphysema, especially for smokers.

# Celery

| CHARACTERISTICS | THE GOOD NEWS FOR YOU |
|---|---|

1) General Information

- Considered a super food for blood pressure.
- High potassium content helps maintain stable blood pressure levels, which in turn improves cardiovascular health.
- Vitamin C boosts the immune system.
- Low in calories, but high in fiber.
- A good source of calcium for healthy bones.
- May lower cholesterol.
- Promotes optimal health.

2) Coumarins

- Enhance the effectiveness of white blood cells in eliminating harmful cells including those that cause cancer.

3) Diuretic

- Stimulates urine production.
- Eliminates excess body fluids.
- Regulates fluid balance in the body.

# Garlic

| CHARACTERISTICS | THE GOOD NEWS FOR YOU |

## CHARACTERISTICS

1) General Information

## THE GOOD NEWS FOR YOU

- Useful antibiotic, which can reduce the risk of heart disease and cancer.
- May minimize stomach ulcers with its powerful sulfate compounds.
- Contains manganese, which may help the body process fatty acids and cholesterol.
- Contains good amounts of vitamin C, which is a powerful antioxidant that protects against free radicals.
- May prevent atherosclerosis and diabetic heart disease and reduce the risk of heart attacks and strokes.

- There are so many health benefits associated with garlic, we can say it's a powerhouse vegetable and it promotes general optimal health.

2) Allicin

- Contains anti-bacterial and anti-viral properties.
- Works together with vitamin C to eliminate harmful microbes.
- Shown to lower blood pressure levels.
- Protects colon cells from toxic substances.

3) Sulfur Compounds

- Contains anti-inflammatory properties.
- Helps control blood pressure by helping blood vessels dilate.
- Decreases bad fats such as cholesterol and triglycerides.

# Green beans

CHARACTERISTICS

1) General Information

2) Folate

THE GOOD NEWS FOR YOU

- Excellent source of vitamin K along with calcium, which help build and maintain healthy bones.
- Contain vitamins C and A, which help provide powerful antioxidants to reduce the number of free radicals in the body.
- Help clean up blood vessels and blocked arteries that will eventually prevent heart attack and stroke.

- Decreases the risk of developing cardiovascular diseases by reducing levels of homocysteine in the blood, which is a major heart attack risk factor.

- Improves nerve function.
- Helps maintain healthy circulation of the blood throughout the body.

3) Vitamin B's

- Vitamin B1 (thiamin), which helps maintain your energy supplies.
- Vitamin B2 (riboflavin), which helps support cellular energy production.
- Vitamin B3 (niacin), which helps in the conversion of the body's fats and proteins into useful energy.
- Vitamin B6, which supports nervous system health.

# Green peas

| CHARACTERISTICS | THE GOOD NEWS FOR YOU |
|---|---|
| **1) General Information** | • Great source of vitamin K, which is essential for healthy bones. <br> • Contain manganese, which helps the body keep cholesterol in check. <br> • Great source of energy boosting vitamin B's. |
| **2) Protein** | • Essential in the muscle building process. <br> • Used by the body to repair and create tissue. <br> • Provides energy for the body to function properly. |
| **3) Lutein/Zeaxanthin** | • Fights eye diseases such as cataracts, which causes the center of eye to become clouded. |

- Protects eyes from free radicals caused by pollution, smoking, or radiation.

4)  Vitamin B's

- Vitamin B1 (thiamin) helps maintain your energy supplies.
- Vitamin B2 (riboflavin) helps support cellular energy production.
- Vitamin B3 (niacin) helps in the conversion of the body's fats, carbohydrates, and proteins into useful energy.
- Vitamin B6 supports nervous system health and promotes proper breakdown of sugars

# Kale/Mustard

## CHARACTERISTICS THE GOOD NEWS FOR YOU

1) General Information

- Contains the highest levels of antioxidants of all vegetables,
- Contains vitamin A, which supports overall vision health.
- High in vitamin C, which boosts the immune system and improves iron absorption.
- Contains manganese content, which helps maintain healthy blood sugar levels.
- Good source of fiber content, which helps keep cholesterol levels in check.

2) Sulforaphane

- Helps repair skin cells from damage caused by exposure to too much UV light.
- Protects against ulcers that form in the stomach.

- Helps clear potential cancerous cells.

3) Lutein/Zeaxanthin

- Fights eye disease such as cataracts and promotes overall eye health.
- Protects eyes from free radicals caused by pollution, smoking, or radiation.

# Mushrooms

CHARACTERISTICS       THE GOOD NEWS FOR YOU

1) General Information

- A great source of copper, which helps in the formation of new blood vessels.
- Powerful source of antioxidants, which protect against oxidative damage to cell structure and DNA.
- Contain tryptophan, which promotes healthy sleep patterns.
- Contains multiple vitamin B contents, which promote energy production— especially vitamin B5, which may help prevent fatigue.
- Good source of protein, which can help in health management.

2) Selenium

- Shown to decrease the odds of developing many types of cancers such as bladder and prostate.
- Plays a role in repairing damaged DNA that can cause cell mutations and eventually cancer.

# Onions

| CHARACTERISTICS | THE GOOD NEWS FOR YOU |
|---|---|
| 1) General Information | |
| | • Contain sulfur compounds that are natural antibiotics offering protection against cancer and heart diseases. |
| | • Help decrease total cholesterol and triglycerides while increasing levels of good cholesterol. |
| | • Promote general heart health and reduces the risk of heart attack and stroke. |
| | • Promote overall digestive health. |
| | • Contain antibacterial properties that may help control colds. |
| 2) Allyl Propyl Sulfoxides | |
| | • Promote healthy blood sugar levels throughout the body. |
| | • For diabetics, help cells respond appropriately to insulin. |

3) Chromium

- Helps reduce total cholesterol and increase the amount of healthy cholesterol available.
- Improves glucose tolerance.
- Helps balance blood sugar levels.

4) Quercetin

- Anti-inflammatory properties.
- Promotes healthy heart function.
- Protects colon cells from cancer-causing substances.
- Works with vitamin C to kill harmful bacteria.

# Romaine lettuce

## CHARACTERISTICS THE GOOD NEWS FOR YOU

1) General Information

- Good source of dietary fiber for digestive health.
- Excellent source of vitamin K for bone structure.
- Contains vitamin A, which helps keep eyes healthy.
- Contains folic acid, which promotes heart and artery health.
- Contains other heart-healthy nutrients including dietary fiber, potassium, calcium, and omega 3 fatty acids.

2) Chromium

- Helps regulate blood sugar levels.
- Helps sensitize cells for absorption purposes.

- Promotes healthy cholesterol levels by increasing levels of good cholesterol and lowering bad cholesterol.

3) Lutein/Zeaxanthin

- Promotes overall vision health.
- Reduces risk of cataracts and age-related eye diseases.
- Protects eyes from free radicals caused by pollution, smoking, or radiation.

# Spinach

| CHARACTERISTICS | THE GOOD NEWS FOR YOU |
|---|---|

1) General Information

- Excellent source of vitamin K, which increases bone density.
- Good source of vitamin A, which helps maintain overall healthy eyes and lungs.
- May reduced risk of various types of cancer.
- Contains vitamin E, which helps protect the brain
- Contains Omega 3 fatty acids, which promote brain health.
- Excellent source of magnesium.

2) Iron

- Spinach offers a large source of iron compared to its calories.
- Iron helps maintain the function of hemoglobin, which carries oxygen throughout the body.

3) Lutein/Zeaxanthin

- One of the most concentrated sources of Lutein/Zeaxanthin.
- Fights against eye disease such as cataracts and promotes vision

4) Tryptophan

- Promotes healthy sleep cycles.
- Helps to regulate your appetite.

5) Folate

- Linked to the prevention of Alzheimer's.
- Promotes cell production, especially for skin health.
- Allows nerves to function properly.
- Reduces the risk of cardiovascular diseases.

# Squash

## CHARACTERISTICS THE GOOD NEWS FOR YOU

1) General Information

- Excellent source of vitamin C, which is a key antioxidant that protects cells and the immune system.
- Contains Omega 3 fatty acids, which help fight inflammation.
- Protein content promotes muscular strength.
- Promotes general bone health because of its calcium, magnesium, and phosphorus nutrients.
- Promotes overall heart health by reducing blood pressure and bad cholesterol.

2) Manganese

- Helps the body metabolize proteins and carbohydrates.
- Helps maintain healthy bones.

- Helps your body synthesize cholesterol.
- Promotes optimal function of your thyroid gland.

3) Beta-Cryptoxanthin

- Protects cells from damaging free radicals.
- Linked to a reduced risk of developing lung cancer and colon cancer.
- May help reduce prostate in men.

# Sweet potatoes

| CHARACTERISTICS | THE GOOD NEWS FOR YOU |
|---|---|

1) General Information

- Sweet potatoes are considered an anti-diabetic food shown to stabilize blood sugar levels and lower insulin resistance.
- Contains high amounts of vitamin A, which protects the lungs against harmful carcinogens, especially those originating from smoking.
- Good source of vitamin C, which is a very powerful antioxidant for protecting cells.

2) Pectin

- Helps manage stress by suppressing hormones in the brain.
- Shown to lower bad cholesterol levels.
- Linked to lower cases of prostate cancer.

3) Beta-Carotene

- Provides a source of vitamin A, which is good for the eyes and the lungs.
- Protects the reproductive system from harmful free radicals.
- Enhances the function of the immune system.
- Unique properties in regulating blood sugar levels

# Tomatoes

| CHARACTERISTICS | THE GOOD NEWS FOR YOU |
|---|---|

1) General Information

- Excellent source of vitamins A & C, which are two powerful antioxidants that contribute to overall health.
- Contains vitamin K, which gives support to the bones.

2) Lycopene

- Protects cells from damage brought on by harmful free radicals.
- Prevents the oxidation of bad cholesterol, which can lead to cardiovascular disease.
- Linked to lower cases of prostate cancer.
- Provides an array of health benefits, especially cancer protection.

3) Potassium

- Helps to regulate blood pressure.
- Reduces the risk of developing kidney stones.
- Helps maintain a healthy calcium level.
- Helps your muscles and nerves function properly.
- Helps enhance food absorption, which in turns contributes to your optimal health.

# BEANS AND GRAINS

# Black beans

CHARACTERISTICS        THE GOOD NEWS FOR YOU

1) General Information

- Promotes overall digestive health.
- Promotes heart health.
- Great source of protein.
- High magnesium content, which is good for preventing heart disease.
- Rich in antioxidant compounds that can help prevent blood clots.
- High fiber content that can help reduce cholesterol.

2) Folate

- Lowers levels of homocysteine in the body, which significantly lowers the risk of a heart attack.
- Improves nerve function.
- Help prevent cardiovascular disease.

- Helps the development of red blood cells, which help carry oxygen throughout the body.

3) Protein

- Needed to maintain healthy skin, hair, and nails.
- Important for maintaining muscle mass, especially in the elderly.
- Essential to keep the body's immune system functioning properly.
- Crucial for body structure.

# Brown Rice

## CHARACTERISTICS

## THE GOOD NEWS FOR YOU

1) General Information

- Good source of fiber, which can help lower blood cholesterol and keep blood sugar levels normal.
- Good source of tryptophan, which is linked to improvement of mood and better sleep.
- Magnesium in brown rice helps keep blood vessels relaxed for easier blood flow.

2) Manganese

- Helps balance blood sugar levels.
- Essential for bone strength.
- Potent antioxidant, which protects cells from free radical damage.
- Helps the body synthesize cholesterol.
- Maintains normal blood sugar levels.

3) Ferulic Acid

- Helps prevent damage caused by free radicals.
- Protects against cell damage caused by radiation.
- Linked to lower blood pressure levels.
- Protects against kidney stones.

# Kidney beans

| CHARACTERISTICS | THE GOOD NEWS FOR YOU |
| --- | --- |

1) General Information

- Rich in both soluble and insoluble fiber, which promotes digestive health.
- Copper and manganese content helps protect body tissue from free radical damage.
- Good source of iron, which helps increase the body's energy.
- Great source of protein.
- May protect against colon cancer.
- High in potassium, which may help control high blood pressure.

2) Folate

- Helps lower levels of homocysteine found in the blood, preventing heart disease.
- Helps prevent anemia.
- Supports the production of red blood cells.

3) Protein

- Used by the body to repair muscle tissue.
- Important for the production of hormones.
- Key for weight management.
- Maintain healthy skin, hair, and nails.

# Lentils

| CHARACTERISTICS | THE GOOD NEWS FOR YOU |
| --- | --- |
| 1) General Information | • Rich in both soluble and insoluble fiber, which helps protect against cardiovascular diseases and cancer.<br>• Soluble fiber helps remove cholesterol from the body.<br>• Insoluble fiber helps prevent constipation.<br>• Good source of protein.<br>• Promotes heart health, improves the flow of blood, oxygen, and nutrients throughout the body. |
| 2) Polyphenolic Phytonutrients | • Powerful source of antioxidants.<br>• Protects the body against free radicals. |

- Enhances the immune response.
- Enhances cell-to-cell communication.

3) Folate

- Helps lower levels of homocysteine, preventing heart disease.
- Improves nerve function.
- Improves overall mental function.

4) Protein

- Used by the body to repair and create tissue.
- Important to build and maintain muscle mass.
- Essential to keep the immune system functioning properly.
- Recommended for weight management.

# Navy beans

| CHARACTERISTICS | THE GOOD NEWS FOR YOU |
|---|---|

1) General Information

- Rich in both soluble and insoluble fiber, which helps to reduce cholesterol.
- High fiber content helps promote overall digestive health.
- Great source of copper and manganese, which help protect cells from free radical damage.
- Potassium found in navy beans helps lower high blood pressure.
- Great source of protein, which helps manage hunger.
- Lowers risk of heart attack.

2) Folate

- Helps lower levels of homocysteine found in the blood, which prevents heart disease.
- Improves nerve function.

- Supports the production of red blood cells.
- Promotes neurological health.
- Helps create cells in the body.

3) Protein

- Used by the body to repair and create tissue.
- Essential to keep immune system functioning properly.
- Key for weight management.
- Last component used by the body to produce energy.

# Oats

| CHARACTERISTICS | THE GOOD NEWS FOR YOU |
|---|---|

1) General Information

- Contain a special fiber called beta-glucan, which helps lower bad cholesterol levels and stabilize blood sugar.
- Manganese content found in oats helps maintain healthy blood sugar levels.
- One of the best grains to keep heart and arteries healthy.
- Polyphenol content helps suppress the growth of tumors.
- Reduce the risk of cardiovascular diseases.

2) Magnesium

- Keeps blood vessels relaxed, thus promoting good heart health.

- Reduces the risk of having a heart attack or stroke.
- Helps give bones their physical structures.
- Helps store fuel in our muscles for muscular development.

3) Avenanthramides

- Contains antioxidants that helps prevent bad cholesterol from oxidizing, which can clog arteries.
- Prevents immune cells from sticking to artery walls, which is the first sign of hardening of the arteries.
- Contains anti-inflammatory properties.

# QUINOA

## CHARACTERISTICS

## THE GOOD NEWS FOR YOU

1) General Information

- Great source of complete protein containing all nine amino acids.
- High in magnesium and manganese, both needed for the maintenance of bone strength and density.
- Great source of dietary fiber, which helps lower bad cholesterol levels and balance blood sugar.
- Promotes cardiovascular health.

2) Protein

- Used by the body to repair and create tissue.
- Key to building muscle.
- Important for a healthy immune system.
- Important for weight management.

3) Iron

- Promotes energy production.
- Needed to transport oxygen to cells in the body.
- Important in the metabolism process.

# Soybeans

| CHARACTERISTICS | THE GOOD NEWS FOR YOU |
|---|---|

### 1) General Information

- High in dietary fiber, which helps keep cholesterol and blood sugar levels in check.
- Good source of protein with hardly any fat, which is great for building and maintaining muscle mass.
- Good source of Omega 3, which can help prevent cancer growth.
- May help reduce symptoms associated with menopause.
- Promotes heart health and may provide benefits for blood pressure.

### 2) Soy Protein

- Helps prevent heart disease.
- Shown to significantly lower bad cholesterol and raise good cholesterol.

- Promotes weight control.
- Great for diabetic patients.

3) Isoflavones

- Reduces the risk of developing breast cancer by keeping estrogen levels under control.
- Lowers the risk of developing prostate cancer.

# Whole wheat

CHARACTERISTICS          THE GOOD NEWS FOR YOU

1) General Information

- High dietary fiber content that promotes digestive health.
- Magnesium helps keep blood vessels functioning properly and helps muscles to relax.
- Promotes balanced blood sugar.
- Contains tryptophan, which promotes better sleep quality.

2) Dietary Fiber

- Helps to balance blood sugar levels, preventing conditions such as diabetes.
- Important for weight management.
- Lowers the risk of developing gallstones.
- Promotes heart health by helping remove excess waste and cholesterol.

3) Manganese

- Helps the body maintain healthy blood sugar levels.
- Provides important antioxidant protection.
- Helps the body process cholesterol and fatty acids.

# HERBS AND SPICES

# Basil

CHARACTERISTICS

THE GOOD NEWS FOR YOU

1) General Information

- Powerful antioxidant.
- Rich in vitamin K, which is needed for the body's healthy blood flow.
- Contains antibiotic and anti-inflammatory properties.
- Contains vitamin C, which gives added protection against free radicals.
- High amounts of iron help the body produce energy.
- Used in remedies for indigestion, nausea, and stomach ache.

2) Orientin/Vicenin

- Protects cell structure from the harmful effects of radiation.
- Provides cell protection against oxidative damage.

3) Eugenol

- Protection against harmful food poisoning bacteria.
- Anti-inflammatory properties that act similarly to aspirin and ibuprofen.

# Cilantro

| CHARACTERISTICS | THE GOOD NEWS FOR YOU |
|---|---|

1) General Information

- Powerful antioxidants for cellular health.
- Great source of vitamin K, which prevents calcium from building up in arteries which can cause cardiovascular issues.
- Promotes heart health by lowering bad cholesterol and increasing good cholesterol.
- Regulates blood sugars, which may help diabetics and people who are insulin resistant.

2) Dodecenal

- Contains anti-bacterial elements that protect against bacteria such as salmonella.
- Shown to be more effective in killing certain bacteria than prescription drugs.

- Tasteless food additive to prevent food-borne illness.

3) Lutein and Zeaxanthin

- Protect against degenerative eye disease.
- Improve overall eye health.

# Cinnamon

| CHARACTERISTICS | THE GOOD NEWS FOR YOU |
|---|---|

1) General Information

- Rich in manganese, which helps maintain normal blood sugar levels.
- Iron content helps in the transportation of oxygen to cells throughout the body.
- Dietary fiber content helps digestion and helps lower bad cholesterol levels.
- Helps indigestion and bloating.
- Helps prevent blood clots.
- Anti-inflammatory protection.

2) Cinnamaldehyde

- Anti-microbial properties give protection against harmful bacteria.
- Prevents blood platelets from clogging, which benefits the body's cardiovascular system.
- May help protect against stroke.

3) Calcium

- Crucial for maintaining bone and teeth strength.
- Prevents osteoporosis, which is a disease that can cause bones to easily fracture.
- Gives structure and strength to bones.
- Helps blood to clot.
- Helps with nerve conduction and muscle contractions.

# Ginger

CHARACTERISTICS         THE GOOD NEWS FOR YOU

1) General Information

- Contains anti-inflammatory and cancer-destroying properties.
- Good source of potassium.
- Ginger is known for its ability to relieve nausea and stomach pain.
- Magnesium content helps control blood sugar and maintains the health of the nervous system.
- Overall digestive aid has the ability to relax digestive track and reduce intestinal gas.

2) Gingerols

- Potent anti-inflammatory.
- Shown to give significant relief to patients with muscular pain and arthritis.

3) Potassium

- Helps control blood pressure levels.

- Important for kidney health; also reduces the risk of developing kidney stones.
- Ensures that the body's blood vessels are working efficiently.
- Helps muscles and nerves to function properly.
- Extremely important in maintaining cellular health.

# Mint

| CHARACTERISTICS | THE GOOD NEWS FOR YOU |
|---|---|

1) General Information

- Improves overall digestive system.
- May help treat depression, stress, and headache.
- Remedy to calm and relax the stomach and indigestion.
- Helps eliminate toxins from the body.
- Good blood cleanser.
- May help with skin health to treat acne, insect's bites, and burns.
- May help with oral health to fight bacteria in the mouth, teeth, and tongue.

2) Menthol

- Offers relief to those with Irritable Bowel Syndrome by relaxing the muscles in the colon.

- Clears congestion in the chest and head during a cold.
- Protects against cancers that develop in the colon, lungs, or on the skin.
- Helps stop the growth of tumors in the pancreas and liver.

# Oregano

| CHARACTERISTICS | THE GOOD NEWS FOR YOU |
| --- | --- |

1) General Information

- Contains more antioxidants than any other herb.
- Demonstrated 42x more antioxidant activity than apples, 30x more than potatoes, 12x more than oranges, and 4x more than blueberries.
- Helps prevent food-poisoning bacteria
- Boosts immune system.
- Vitamin K content helps prevent arteries from hardening.
- Great source of dietary fiber, which is important for digestive health.
- May help lower cholesterol.

2) Thymol/Carvacrol

- Anti-bacterial properties shown to stop the growth of harmful bacteria.
- Provides antioxidant protection.

# Parsley

| CHARACTERISTICS | THE GOOD NEWS FOR YOU |
|---|---|

1) General Information

- High in vitamin C to boost the immune system.
- Excellent source of vitamin K, which helps protect bones from fracturing and helps protect against blood clots.
- Contains essential oils used as traditional remedy for pain, fluid retention, and cramps.
- Contains a strong antioxidant property that prevents cell damage.
- Good source of iron for energy production.

2) Essential Oils

- Help neutralize harmful carcinogens from smoking and other harmful substances.

- Work as an antioxidant protecting the body's cells from damage caused by oxidation.

3) Folate

- Essential for the healthy production of red blood cells.
- Helps suppress levels of homocysteine, a substance linked to heart disease in the blood steam.
- Promotes cell production.

# Rosemary

## CHARACTERISTICS

### 1) General Information

## THE GOOD NEWS FOR YOU

- Provide powerful antioxidant for overall cellular health.
- Dietary fiber helps digestion and improves colon health.
- Iron helps in the production of energy.
- Good source of calcium, which is essential to maintain healthy bones and teeth.
- Rosemary is used to boost memory.
- Promotes liver detoxification.
- Can fight symptoms of cold, flu, and rheumatism.

2) Rosmarinic Acid

- Provides antioxidant protection against free radicals.
- Reduces inflammation.

# Sage

## CHARACTERISTICS

## THE GOOD NEWS FOR YOU

1) General Information

- Has the most antioxidant effects found in herbs.
- Linked to increased memory.
- Sage has a strong anti-bacterial and anti-inflammatory effect.
- Used for throat infections and gastrointestinal problems.
- Relieves hot flashes in many menopausal women.

2) Cholesterol

- Reduces bad cholesterol.
- Increases good cholesterol.
- Increases antioxidant activity in the blood system.

# Thyme

| CHARACTERISTICS | THE GOOD NEWS FOR YOU |
| --- | --- |

1) General Information

- High in vitamin K, which protects bones from fracture and prevents calcium buildup in arteries.
- Strong antioxidant action.
- Rich in flavonoids, which protect against age related diseases.
- Iron content found in thyme helps transport oxygen throughout the body.
- Manganese protects cells against free radicals.

2) Thymol

- Anti-bacterial properties shown to stop the growth of harmful bacteria.
- Protects against food poisoning caused by staphylococcus and E.coli.

- Boosts the effects of Omega 3 fatty acids.
- Increases the amount of healthy fat in cells.
- Promotes healthy brain functions.

# Turmeric

| CHARACTERISTICS | THE GOOD NEWS FOR YOU |
|---|---|

1) General Information

- Anti-inflammatory properties comparable to prescription and over-the-counter medicine.
- Excellent source of iron, which helps transport oxygen to cells in the body and to boost energy.
- Potassium content helps control blood pressure.
- Helps people with joint disease.

2) Curcumin

- Powerful anti-inflammatory shown to give relief to those with rheumatoid arthritis.

- Shown to be just as effective as prescription anti-inflammatory medicine.
- Reduces morning stiffness and joint swelling.

3) Manganese

- Protects cells against free radical damage.
- Helps the body maintain healthy blood sugar levels.
- Needed for the thyroid gland to function properly.

# SEEDS AND NUTS

# Almonds

| CHARACTERISTICS | THE GOOD NEWS FOR YOU |
|---|---|

1) General Information

- Known as the "king of nuts" for its high nutritional value.
- Excellent source of vitamin E, which protects against cancer and cardiovascular disease.
- Contains dietary fiber, which promotes digestive health.
- High source of monounsaturated fat, which is important for a healthy heart.
- Great source of calcium that supports bones and nerve functions.

2) Manganese

- Helps maintain proper blood sugar levels.

- Protects the quality of the body's nerves.
- Helps eliminate free radicals.
- Helps your body synthesize cholesterol.

3) Vitamin E

- Protects skin from harmful UV light.
- Helps protect cells against free radical damage.
- Protects against cancer and cardiovascular disease.
- Prevents bad cholesterol from oxidizing, which is the first sign of arthrosclerosis (hardening of the arteries).

4) Magnesium

- Helps keep blood pressure stable.
- Helps maintain bone strength.
- Promotes the production of energy.

# Cashews

| CHARACTERISTICS | THE GOOD NEWS FOR YOU |
|---|---|

1) General Information

- Contain high amounts of magnesium, which is important for bone and heart health.
- High in zinc, which gives a boost to the immune system.
- Great source of vitamin B, which provides the body with energy.
- Monounsaturated fats protect the heart from disease.

2) Copper

- Supports joint integrity.
- Important for the production of melanin, which is responsible for skin and hair pigment.
- Essential for energy production.

3) Phytosterols

- Helps block bad cholesterol absorption in the body.
- Lowers bad cholesterol levels.

- Protection for heart and arterial diseases.

4) Oleic Acid

- Healthy monounsaturated fats promote heart health.
- Shown to lower bad cholesterol and raise healthy cholesterol levels.
- Lowers the risk of developing breast cancer.
- Help reduce high triglyceride levels.

# Cocoa beans

## CHARACTERISTICS

## THE GOOD NEWS FOR YOU

1) General Information

- Monounsaturated fats improve heart health.
- Magnesium content helps protect the heart.
- Fiber content helps remove cholesterol from the body.
- Promote overall cardiovascular health.

2) Proanthocyanidin

- Provides anti-inflammatory benefits.
- Protects the body against free radicals.
- Helps prevent bad cholesterol from oxidizing, which can lead to heart problems.

3) Caffeine

- Boosts energy levels.
- Improves concentration.

4) Iron

- May increases memory.

- Helps maintain the proper function of hemoglobin, which carries oxygen from the lungs to cells throughout the body.
- Helps the body produce energy.

## Flaxseeds

CHARACTERISTICS          THE GOOD NEWS FOR YOU

1)  General Information

- Great source of fiber, which is important for the colon, and also balances cholesterol levels.
- The most concentrated plant source of the Omega 3 fatty acids.
- Promote overall heart and digestive health.

2)  Omega 3 Fatty Acids

- High in Omega 3 content, linked to fewer cases of Alzheimer's disease.
- Help prevent cognitive decline due to aging.
- Improve blood flow throughout the body.
- Anti-inflammatory properties.

3)  Manganese

- Helps maintain proper blood sugar levels.

- Helps the body process fatty acids and cholesterol.
- Protects the quality of the body's nerves.

4) Lignan

- Lowers the risk of developing breast cancer.
- Reduces the rate of hair loss and increases rate of hair regeneration.
- Helps prevent cardiovascular disease.

# Peanuts

CHARACTERISTICS          THE GOOD NEWS FOR YOU

1)  General Information

- Great source of protein, which helps build muscle and control hunger.
- Manganese helps fight off free radicals.
- Contains properties that lower the risk of cardiovascular diseases.
- Folate reduces homocysteine found in blood which helps prevent heart disease.

2)  Resveratrol

- Provides antioxidant protection.
- Decreases the risk of developing heart disease.
- Contains anti-inflammatory properties.
- Protects arteries from hardening, which can lead to a heart attack.

3)  Vitamin E

- Provides cells with antioxidant protection.
- Important for the health of the heart and arteries.
- Boosts brain power.
- Reduces the risk of having a stroke or heart attack.

4) Niacin

- Protects against cognitive decline due to the effects of aging.
- Stabilizes blood sugar levels.
- Helps lower cholesterol levels.

# Pumpkin seeds

| CHARACTERISTICS | THE GOOD NEWS FOR YOU |
|---|---|

1) General Information

- Good source of zinc, which is essential for a healthy immune system.
- Great source of protein for muscular health.
- High in iron which is important for preventing fatigue.
- Help remove bad cholesterol from the body and help prevent, breast, colon, and prostate cancer.
- Promote flexibility in bones and joint health.

2) Manganese

- Helps maintain proper blood sugar levels.
- Protects the quality of the body's nerves.
- Helps eliminate free radicals.

3) Cucurbitacins

- Helps prevent and treat an enlarged prostate by slowing down the production of prostate cells in the body.
- Promotes overall men's health.

4) Magnesium

- Helps in the production of energy.
- Important for controlling inflammation.
- Reduces the risk of having a heart attack.

# Sesame seeds

| CHARACTERISTICS | THE GOOD NEWS FOR YOU |
|---|---|

1) General Information

- Good source of dietary fiber for digestion.
- High in tryptophan, which promotes healthy sleep patterns.
- Great source of calcium, which promotes bone health.
- Good source of copper as an antioxidant for cellular health.

2) Copper

- Improves blood cell elasticity.
- Helps the formation of new blood vessels.
- Important for healthy skin and joints.
- Anti-inflammatory action, reducing pain, and swelling.

3) Manganese

- Keeps bones healthy and strong.
- Promotes energy production.

- Protects cells from free radical damage.

4) Lignan

- Increases vitamin E supplies.
- Protects the liver from the effects of oxidation.
- Shown to reduce bad cholesterol levels.
- Contains anti-inflammatory properties.

# Sunflower seeds

CHARACTERISTICS

THE GOOD NEWS FOR YOU

1) General Information

- Excellent source of vitamin E.
- Great source of magnesium.
- Plays an important role in brain health.
- Contains folate, which helps with brain function.
- Rich in plant sterols, which helps lower cholesterol.

2) Vitamin E

- Contains significant anti-inflammatory properties.
- Contains antioxidants, which helps protect cell membranes against free radical damage.
- Plays an important role in the prevention of cardiovascular diseases and with protection from colon cancer.

3) Thiamin

- Helps the body convert food into energy.
- Ensures that the nervous system is functioning properly.
- Helps with the skin, hair, liver, and eyes.

4) Manganese

- Helps maintain balanced blood pressure.
- Reduces the risk of heart attack and stroke.
- Promotes healthy bones and energy production.

# Walnuts

## CHARACTERISTICS

## THE GOOD NEWS FOR YOU

1) General Information

- Excellent source of Omega 3 fatty acids.
- Monosaturated fat (healthy fat) improves heart health by lowering cholesterol.
- Great source of copper, which is important for bone health.
- Rich in manganese which helps eliminate free radicals.
- May increase the elasticity of the arteries.

2) Omega 3 Fatty Acids

- Known for their high content of Omega fatty acids.
- Provide anti-inflammatory benefits.
- Lower levels of bad fats (cholesterol and triglycerides).
- Defend the body against cardiovascular disease.

3) Ellagic Acid

- Protects cells from free radical damage.
- Detoxifies potential cancer-causing substances in the body.
- Helps stop the replication of cancer cells.

# CHAPTER 7

# PERSONAL FINANCE

I have two Bachelor degrees. The first, which is in Business Administration with a minor in Entrepreneurship, is from the University of Florida; the second, from Florida Atlantic University, is in Accounting. I spend most of my time helping people with their finances, so I've looked forward to writing this chapter.

What I am about to teach you isn't taught in colleges and universities. What I am about to teach you has been acquired by dealing with hundreds of clients, working with corporations, taking extra classes, and attending numerous seminars, all regarding finances.

There are 4 elements at the foundation of personal finance that are essential in order for you to do well:

1. Behavior
2. Budget/Cash Flow Planning
3. Personal Financial Statement/Balance Sheet
4. Ratio Analysis

## Behavior

Money is a tool of exchange that applies to every single part of your life and therefore must be taken very seriously:

➤ Housing
➤ Food
➤ Transportation
➤ Entertainment
➤ Charitable Giving
➤ Child expense
➤ And on and on …

Therefore, you being serious—your behavior—is of utmost importance when it comes to your personal finances. And, the good news is, once you start taking your personal finance seriously, it will affect your behavior in every single aspect of your life.

*Behavior always comes before finances.* Every asset or liability (debt) you acquire during your lifetime is mostly because of your behavior.

Check this out:

➤ For the average person:

## BEHAVIOR
## COMES BEFORE
## FINANCIAL PLANNING

There is nothing wrong with that model. A good majority of the assets or liabilities or debt you acquire during your lifetime is because of your behavior. Now, if you don't know the difference between an asset and a liability you might be in big financial trouble.

➤ For a more financially sophisticated and savvy individual:

## FINANCIAL PLANNING
## COMES BEFORE
## BEHAVIOR

Remember the example we used earlier that goes: "In the beginning God created the heavens and the earth"? Those who are "bent" toward financial maturity are those who sit down and create their sources of income, knowing fully how they are going to earn their money. Personally, I wish I'd known this before graduating from college; it would have totally changed my view about earning money.

### Budget/Cash Flow Planning

My dad is an entrepreneur. I started to work for him at a very early age—every summer, before going on vacation or to summer camp. —He would say, "As an entrepreneur, you don't need a budget, because it will restrict you." Hearing this over and over, I grew up thinking this was correct.

I graduated from college, worked in a corporation, and opened my own business … all without using a budget. As a matter of fact, I hated the word budget. I thought that a "budget" was for average people, people who didn't have self-control, people who will buy things on credit and pay the minimum balance at the end of each month, etc.

But about two or three years ago, I changed my opinion.

I had just broken up with my girlfriend and I was discouraged because I had put so much effort and emotion into that relationship and it hadn't worked out. After one year of being with her, which was the longest I'd ever been in a romantic relationship, I knew I'd have to start from scratch in a new relationship with someone else.

Having more time, I decided to focus all my attention on my business. Up until then, my business was doing okay, but I wanted to *seriously* grow my income. I purchased audio-books by couple of motivational speakers. The first one was *The Secret of the Millionaire Mind: Mastering the Inner Game of Wealth* by T. Harv Eker. This is a good book filled with good great philosophies, but there is a great sentence that totally caught me off guard. He said, "Your income will only grow to the extent that you do."

This is when I started to think about a budget. After all, I hear the word "budget" all the time. I figured there might be something I didn't know about it.

Then I took the Dave Ramsey course, *Financial Peace University.* I started to understand the concept of "budgeting."

Now, even though the book and the course are great educational tools, both which helped me to eventually establish a budget, they were not the main reason I did. My main reason for starting a budget was the **sensation of emptiness and the fact that I had to start over from scratch.**

You may think this doesn't make sense. "Gee is crazy and he has no idea of what he's talking about." But allow me the chance to connect the dots.

When I was in the relationship with my ex-girlfriend, we went out to dinner, we double-dated with our best friends, we held hands, and we told each other intimate stories. We went clubbing, spent time with each other's families, we gave and received support when needed, and we cared for one another. It was nice to have someone to go places with and to hear, "You two are such a cute couple. You look so good together."

We all know that relationships require:

> ➢ Lots of time
> ➢ Emotions
> ➢ Personal attention
> ➢ Money
> ➢ Tolerance
> ➢ And so much more …

Now let's go back to the finance world. Here are just a few examples of what money can buy:

| New Cellular | Go to Europe | Ipad | Stock portfolio |
|---|---|---|---|
| House | Shoes | Movies | Shopping |
| New Car | Surgeries | Groceries | Real estate |
| Fine cuisine | Fine clothing | Make up | Travel |
| Watch | Computer | Sporting goods | Hire people |
| Jewelries | Games tickets | Rims | Skin care |
| Businesses | VIP reservation | Music | Video games |

| Vacation to the Caribbean | Books | Concerts | Adult entertainment |
|---|---|---|---|
| Perfume | Suit | Camera | Barbecue Grill |
| Beach front properties | Furniture | Appliances | Education |
| Exotic foods | Motorcycle | Sun glasses | Jet sky |
| Flat screen TV | Luxury condo | Kitchen remodeling | Ice cream |
| Home décor | Investments | Medication | Chocolate |

Now remember that money is a medium tool for exchange. If you don't live under a budget, as money comes in you will spend it. The more money that comes in, the more you will spend.

If you are good at what you do, here is what's going to happen: the more money you earn over time, the more money you will spend at things you think you need for happiness.

Now put this picture in your mind: Imagine that you own a garden and that your job is to water the garden in order for the foliage to grow. You can either water the plants enough for them to grow and harvest a beautiful garden or you can water your garden so much you will eventually kill all the plants. With the previous example, we have the following analogy: Imagine the water is your money and the few plants in your garden are the few things in life that bring you joy and happiness. If your water hose is out of control, you are going to water the plants so much; your garden will eventually end up a flooded garden.

When it comes to budget, you will spend most of your money on a bunch of different things, which will eventually kill the few things you really enjoy because now you have too many distractions. Your plant only needed a little bit of water in order to grow.

Sometimes the things that make us the happiest don't require that much money, but they do require constant nurturing. If you watered your plants properly and took great care of them, in the morning you can wake and look at a beautiful garden or even pick some fruits from the vine. But if your garden is flooded, you will be unhappy and unable to enjoy it. The same thing with your money; if you spend your money wisely on the things you enjoy, one day you will reap the benefits of your work.

Now let me connect the dots between my relationship and the budget.

Being in a breakup is one of the most painful things one can go through. I've seen and heard some ugly things in my own family, among friends, clients and co-workers. So, allow me to associate the words "breakup" and "divorce" with a few other words that can illustrate my point:

➢ Hell
➢ Ugliness
➢ Backstabbing
➢ Misery
➢ Agony
➢ Excessive pain

The same way I left my previous relationship feeling empty and then had to start again from scratch, well, that's the same way I spent a lot of my time and money on different things in my life. Then, come to find out, the things that I truly enjoyed were the things I neglected. So, with them, I had to start again from scratch. If you've ever been in a breakup, associate the pain you felt with the "pain" of not having a budget that works.

I've been always a fan of music. As a matter of fact, when I was in my teens, I called a friend of mine and said, "Let's start a band." And we did. We started a small band. We spent hours practicing and playing our favorite songs. Then college came and I had to make a choice — be a musician or go to college.

I decided to go to college.

After graduation and after I started working, I still had a deep desire to continue playing the guitar. I decided to play in the music department at a church. In time, I left that church and, in time, I stop practicing my guitar. Between work, having my own business, dating, and my family, I got side-tracked. The guitar went untouched, unnoticed, and often times un-dusted.

About a month ago, I entered the store where I purchased my first guitar. I almost cried. That deep sense of sorrow came upon me. I realized that a portion of my life had passed without me playing and I literally had to start again from scratch.

I am not a parent, therefore I don't have the experience or the qualifications to give advice, but ...

I used to work with a woman who told me that she'd rather stay late at work instead of going home to be with her kids. This wasn't a onetime situation either. Week after week would go by in which I saw her stay at work instead of going home. Clearly something was wrong. Now there may have been a lot of reasons for her behavior, but I was left to wonder if she might have a budget problem. Maybe she needed the money from the job in order to feed her kids. Or maybe she had spoiled the kids so much, she now had no control over them. Or perhaps the house she lived in didn't have enough space or the commodity to handle the number of kids she had. Maybe she promised the kids something (food, toys ...) and couldn't keep to her promises because she had no money. Or, maybe she's "running away from home" because she pushed her husband away and now she cannot face her responsibility as the sole earner of the house and raising her kids alone.

Whatever the situation was, I highly doubt she gave birth to her children so she could stay away from them.

Here is the point I want to make: We all have the same amount of time in a day. Twenty-four hours. And we have limited choices of the things we can do in that period with our time and money. So stay focused on the things that truly matter to you and spend money on the things that truly matter to you.

In summary, here is couple of reasons that illustrate the importance of a budget:

➤ Having a budget helps us avoid the sensation of emptiness.
➤ Having a budget helps us use our time more effectively and efficiently for the things that matters to us.
➤ Having a budget helps us restrict ourselves from foolishness and from attracting unnecessary problems.
➤ Having a budget helps us save money faster.
➤ Having a budget prevents us from making quick decisions (decision that are based on impulse instead of rational thinking) and allows us time to know ourselves better and make better decisions.
➤ Having a budget helps us accumulate long-term values and equities.
➤ Having a budget helps us invest money in order to accomplish a bigger goal.
➤ Having a budget helps us avoid stress, headaches, and other physical ailments.
➤ Having a budget helps us become more creative and manage what we already possess more effectively and efficiently.
➤ Having a budget helps us to find real happiness and long-lasting joy.

### Personal Financial Statement/Balance Sheet

A fundamental in finance is a personal financial statement, something everyone should have, including children.

A personal financial statement is the measurement of finances, listing every asset and liability acquired in a lifetime. A personal financial statement will indicate if you've been "good" or "bad" with money and will tell you, once you have retired, if you acquired more assets or liabilities during the time you worked.

- **Definitions**

**Asset**: Something someone has acquired or purchased, and that has monetary value (its cost, book value, market value, or residual value). For example, an asset can be something physical, such as cash, a business, stock portfolio, land, car, shoes, jewelry …

**Liability**: An obligation that legally binds an individual or a company to settle a debt. When one is *liable* for a debt, they are responsible for paying the debt. A **liability** can mean something that is a hindrance or puts an individual or group at a disadvantage, or something that someone is responsible for paying or settling. Examples of liabilities include: debts, mortgages, car payments, school loans, outstanding credit card debts …

**Net worth**: All your assets minus all your liabilities. In other words everything you own, minus everything you owe.

I didn't have a personal financial statement until I was 27. This is, in my opinion, very bad, because I technically started to work when I was 7. I always thought what is in your bank account determined your net worth. Twenty years of working on and off and I didn't have a proper measure to let me know how I was doing financially.

As a professional, I think the following questions are worth asking:

> How many classes did you take in your lifetime in which you were not required to pass a test so see if you learned the material?

> Have you ever driven your car for more than a month without looking at the gas gage?

> ➤ After you have gotten ready to go somewhere, do you usually look at yourself in the mirror to make sure everything is fine?

I bet you answered "yes, yes, and yes." So then why in the world would you let a month pass without looking at your personal financial statement?

Why every month? Because if you do, you will fall under the law of focus. The more you pay attention to your personal financial statement, the more action you will take toward improving your finances.

Two things you must do to become financially "free" and secure:

1. **GET** out of debt and **STAY** out of debt.
2. Your "income-producing assets" should represent 30% to 80% of all your assets

It's that simple.

### 1. Get Out of Debt and Stay Out of Debt

Originally, all I knew about debt was that if you don't have the money to pay the full balance of your credit card, don't buy on credit. This is what I call "limited thinking."

Personal debt is a real problem. A serious problem, because **personal debt reduces your net worth.** Period.

Remember the formula that says: **Assets – Liability = Net Worth**? Well, it's better to live by the following formula: **Assets = Net Worth**. In other words, it's better to have *no* liabilities.

The best advice I can give you is this: ***get out of debt and stay out of debt***.

It's always good to seek counsel from people that are wiser than you, so if you don't fully believe me, please read the following:

*The rich rule over the poor, and the borrower is the slave of the lender* (Proverbs 22:7 NIV). *Let no debt remain outstanding* (Romans 13:8 NIV).

*It's God's will for you to live in prosperity instead of poverty. It's God's will for you to pay your bills and not be in debt (Joel Osteen).*

*Rather go to bed supper less than rise in debt* (Benjamin Franklin).

*Debt is dumb; cash is king* (Dave Ramsey).

*More smart people have gone broke through leverage* [borrowing or debt] *than through any other activity. A smart person can't go broke unless they use leverage. It just doesn't make any sense.* (Warren Buffet/ http://www.youtube.com/watch?v=v_96Mnm0jtk).

Mr. Buffet also said, "Good business or investment decisions will eventually produce quite satisfactory economic results, with no aid from leverage. It seems to us both foolish and improper to risk what is important … for some extra returns that are relatively unimportant." (http://www.buffettsecrets.com/warren-buffett-debt.htm)

If you are starting a business and you need capital to get it going, there is nothing wrong with borrowing money, but you will want to pay it back as soon as possible. If you can avoid borrowing, avoid it, but borrowing money for this reason is okay. However, the following two conditions should apply:

➢ You Are *Starting* a Business ...

... Not *running* a business. For example, let's say you are a mechanic and you want to start a "traveling" business where you go to the clients who need your help with auto repair. But, you need a portable box of tools. Is it okay to obtain a loan from a bank or from investors? Yes. But, within one year you should be able to fully pay that debt and start accumulating cash for future investments. Now, let's say you have done this and you want to expand and have your own garage. I suggest that you do this with your *own* cash. So many businesses start borrowing money and keep on borrowing money for expansion, product development, location, etc. You want to make sure that the philosophy of running your business is based on *having* cash instead of borrowing over and over again. An alternative, if you really need additional cash to expand, is to find investors.

➢ Keep business, business.

If you do decide to borrow money, make sure it's done in a business environment and in the name of your business and not in your personal name. Your business is not *you*. You have your own social security number and the business should have its own tax ID. Don't mix the two up.

**2. Make 30-80% of your assets "income producing assets"**

There are different kinds of assets, but the key to financial success is to have 30-80% of your assets be *income*-producing assets. Here are a few examples of *non*-income producing assets:

- Personal residence
- Cars
- Household furnishings
- Personal goods (such as shoes, watches, TV)

Here are a few examples of *income*-producing assets:

- Personal business
- Rental properties
- Business Partnerships Interest
- Stocks

- **Factors to keep in mind in regards "income-producing assets":**

➤ Investments Control

This is very important. Let's say you manage your own business. This means *you* take the risk for the business and you should have an idea how the money is made and spent. It is at your discretion to hire people, invest in equipment, introduce new products and services, etc. At the end of the day, *you* control the investment.

You can also invest in assets you do *not* control, for example, buying stock in a company. Stockholders don't necessarily have control on the day-to-day decisions of the corporation. Therefore you have to be cautious and do your due diligence before investing a penny. There are a lot of predators out there who are looking to get your money. Sometimes those predators are family members, friends, co-workers, etc. This is what Bernie Madoff did; he stole billions of dollars from investors. So do your research.

Before you invest your money in any type of vehicle or business that you do not have control over, make sure you do the following:

- Only invest an amount you are comfortable losing if worse comes to worse.
- Know and understand your investment.
- Put everything in writing.
- Make certain the financial reporting of companies you invest in are done by an independent Certified Public Accounting firm.

- Don't invest with your emotions. Make sure you do a background check, history check, etc., and ask for references regarding the people who will be managing your money.

➤ Active income

Active income simply means that you have to participate in the effort in order to get paid. If you work, you get paid. If you don't work, you don't get paid. Active income is good, but if you want to become financially independent (the ability to live on the income produced by your personal resources and assets), your income source cannot come only from active income. Financial independence requires that your assets produce enough cash flow to sustain your lifestyle without you having to work.

➤ Passive income

Simply put, passive income is when you receive income without having to participate in the operation of that income. A couple of examples are:

- Rental income from properties
- Dividend from stocks
- Licensing a software
- Franchising a food recipe
- Systems from your own business

Last year I traveled from Florida to Atlanta just for few days and I wanted to park in the airport or near the airport. This way when I get back from Atlanta, I could just take my car and leave the airport without having to wait for anyone. I went to a parking website and I was able to reserve a parking spot at a hotel near the airport for less than half of the amount that the airport parking was charging. That website charged me $2 for the processing fee. So instead of paying $65 at the airport I only paid $24. Amazing deal.

Now let's be conservative and illustrate this service throughout the United States:

| Travelers | Odds of Using Service | Airports | Processing Fee | Daily Income |
|-----------|------------------------|----------|----------------|--------------|
| 3500 | 2% | 50 | $2 | $7,000 |

This is a great business model. I guarantee you the people that put that business together thought through their financials before their behavior. Their target was *passive* income and not *active* income.

- **Other Financial Factors**
  - ➤ Liquidity

Liquidity simply means cash. Money you have in the bank or money market account. We also can define liquidity as cash available to purchase or create investments classified as income-generating assets. Always keep this sentence in your mind: "Cash is king."

Also keep inflation in mind, even though "cash is king," generally speaking $1 today is worth less a year from now. That's why people buy commodities such as gold and silver.

  - ➤ Personal residence

Your personal residence is not an income-producing asset; it takes money out of your pocket every month through:
- Utilities
- Maintenance
- Mortgage
- Association fees
- Real estate taxes

Therefore I strongly recommend living in a place you can afford and your combined housing payments (everything listed above) are less than 25% of your income.

➢ Non income-producing assets

Non income-producing assets, such as personal goods, should be in the lower percentage class of assets in your personal financial statements. This is important to know because:

## RETURN ON INVESTMENT (ROI) = $0 FOR NON INCOME-PRODUCING ASSETS

In other words, if you had used the money you spent on *those* assets on income-producing assets instead, you would have had some return on your investment. That's why it's so important and crucial to create and monitor your personal financial statement.

### Ratio Analysis

This section is in percentages because I believe whatever your income is, it should more or less follow a percentage-based system for the following items in your budget:

1. Church and charitable giving: Minimum 10% - Maximum 15%
2. Entertainment: Minimum 5% - Maximum 15%
3. Investments: Minimum 10% (and up to 60%)
4. Housing: Less than 25% of income
5. *Healthy Financials Improvements: Less than 20%*
6. Education: Less than 15%

Let's look at each of the sections:

### 1) Church and charitable giving: Minimum 10%-Maximum 15%

➢ For unbelievers:

I was listening to an excellent motivational speaker, Jim Rhon, who made an interesting comment regarding giving. He said, "The process of receiving starts by giving." There is also this amazing little book by Bob Burg called *"The Go-Giver: A little Story About a Powerful Business Idea"* that clearly explain this point.

Allow me to illustrate this by using my accounting practice. Whenever I am prospecting a new client, I first give:

- My time (I take time to go see that client and convince them that I have a good service to provide.)
- My Shared Experience (I tell them about my experiences with previous clients and show them how I can solve their problems.)
- My Discount (I usually discount the price of my services in order to earn their business.)

Generally I have to go through all that in order to earn their business. In return, I get monetary value. But without me giving *first*, more than likely, I wouldn't get much.

It's the same principle for money; if you keep an open hand and give money for good causes, the universe will make sure you get more money in your hand to keep sharing.

➢ For believers:

This principle is called "tithing." Whether you believe in it or not, allow me to explain to you why you should tithe. Let me start by saying that God doesn't need your money and tithing is not part of the Ten Commandments. Tithing is voluntary. When you tithe, you should find a good church (storehouse) to bring your tithes to. Especially today when the church has more work than ever to do in:

- Creating disciples
- Fighting hunger
- Helping to stop sex-slavery
- Creating housing for orphans
- Working to restore broken marriages/families
- Helping to reinstate former addicts into the labor force
- Helping to create men and women of integrity through services and education

- Helping to reduce gang violence
- Helping to bring encouragement to the hopeless
- And so much more…

Once you begin participating in tithing, you are fueling God's business (the restoration and reconciliation of his created world. In the Bible we read in the book of Revelation — *Then I saw "a new heaven and a new earth," for the first heaven and the first earth had passed away….. God will wipe every tear from their eyes. There will be no more death or mourning or crying or pain, for the old order of things has passed away."* (Revelation 21:1-4 NIV)

I believe that if you earn your money justly and honestly, you have placed yourself into a unique position, not only for others and the kingdom of God, but for yourself as well.

Here are six ways in which tithing becomes beneficial to *you*:

1. When it comes to giving, your conscience will be clear. With tithing, your conscience is clear with God because you are advancing his kingdom.

2. Your productivity will increase in greater ways than you can imagine. Once you start giving your "first fruits," you become less self-centered and more productive and fruitful.

3. You will receive protection from above. According to the book of Malachi 3: 10-11 (NIV), the Lord has said, "Bring the whole tithe into the storehouse, that there may be food in my house. Test me in this … and see if I will not throw open the floodgates of heaven and pour out so much blessing that there will not be room enough to store it. I will prevent pests from devouring your crops, and the vines in your fields will not drop their fruit before it is ripe".

4. You will tap into God's endless power. Throughout the Scriptures, the only time God instructs us to "test" Him is in Malachi 3:10 (see above). **"TEST ME"** He says, **"and see if I will not throw open the floodgates of heaven and**

**pour out so much blessing that there will not be room enough to store it.**"

5. You will obtain a more hopeful attitude. If God says he will "open the floodgates ..." then you should wake up every day, excited to receive God's blessings.

6. Your income and responsibility will increase. Not only will God meet all your needs (food, shelter, clothing ...), but He will also increase your income as well *when* you position yourself to receive more of His blessings. *You have been faithful with a few things, I will put you in charge of many things* (Matthew 25:21 NIV). *Whoever has will be given more, and they will have an abundance. Whoever does not have, even what he has will be taken from him* (Matthew 13:12 NIV).

The reason I don't suggest giving more than 15% to a church is because God is looking for a return on the talents He gave you. In other words, you need to be a steward to what He gave you and multiply it until His return.

In April of this year (2013), I was fortunate to go on a four-day vacation to the Bahamas. On my way there I picked up a book called *Living in Financial Victory*, by Dr. Tony Evans, and it's so far one of the best books I read this year. When I returned from the trip, I also purchased an awesome six-CD audio set by Pastor James MacDonald entitle "God's Money." These authors opened my mind when it comes to the concept of stewardship. In both teachings, they quote the following passage from the Bible: *[Jesus] said, "A man of noble birth went to a distant country to have himself appointed king and then to return. So he called ten of his servants and gave them ten minas. 'Put this money to work,' he said, 'until I come back.'"* (Luke 19:12 NIV)

Instead of giving more than 15% of your income, the overflow, or extra money, that remains should be invested in your "gifts, talents, family education, and businesses." In this way, in the future when you give, your 10-15% will be worth even more.

## 2) Entertainment: Minimum 5%-Maximum 15%

I believe that entertainment should be the second line on your budget list after tithing. Why? Because there is no way I am going to properly behave if I don't enjoy at least a little of my life.

The movie *Jerry Maguire* (with Tom Cruise and Cuba Gooding, Jr.) gave us a lot of quotable lines, among them, "Show me the money." I feel the same way about entertainment. *Show me the entertainment.* With a reasonable amount of entertainment money (about 5-15% income), I can fashion fun activities during the month. In this way, I keep myself and my life in "balance." Which is a key concept for success.

Regarding entertainment: 15% is your maximum. A lot of people overdo it with entertainment. As your income increases, so does your amount for entertainment. A key principle here is contentment. You must be content with what you have. If you only have $100 for entertainment for the month, be content with that amount and fashion some activities to fit that number. This might surprise you a little bit coming from a financial guy. But, for me, I hate it when I listen to a financial speaker and all they tell you to do with your money is "save, save, and save." (Please note, I am not talking about *investing*. I am talking about having your money in a low-interest savings account.). In my opinion that's not too smart. I am sorry but I am an investor, not a saver.

Why? First of all, because you only have one life to live. Not two, three or four. Only one.

Don't tell me to save all my money for when I am old. Tomorrow is not promised. Secondly, the odds of death are 10 out of 10. You came in this world with nothing, and you will leave with nothing. You cannot take anything with you. Why should I keep on saving constantly if I cannot leave earth with my stuff?

Therefore it's really wise to see ourselves as stewards of the things we currently manage in this lifetime.

This might sound very stupid but it's true. You can't even leave planet earth with your favorite cheese burger in your stomach (You don't know when you are going to die). Earlier we spoke about Warren Buffet and he's known as the world greatest money maker. His philosophy about money is to give all his fortune away when he passes away for philanthropic purposes. Interesting thought.

The mentality of saving, saving and saving leaves you broke and unfulfilled in my opinion. You are leaving your money in a savings account at the bank so that they can make all the returns on *your* "money."

### 3) Investments: Minimum 10% (and up to 60%)
Here is a reasonable formula:

➢ Savings

You should have at least 18-24 months of emergency funds in cash. Let's say you have a budget of $2000/month. Make sure you have $36,000 to $48,000 in cash at all times. Please keep in mind that this amount is an emergency fund (For example: hospitalization, or an accident that prohibits work for a period, etc.). It cannot be used for any special project such as sending your kids to college or a down payment for a new house.

➢ Invest, invest, and invest

Even if you invest in an item with moderate risk, you will get a better return than from a savings account at the bank. Remember what I said regarding investments earlier. Make sure to store large amounts of cash that allow you to buy or create larger investments with a better ROI. The minimum investment amount is 10% of your income. More or less this investment will assure you a fixed income when you are advanced in age and cannot work as much as you used to. More importantly, please notice that in my budget recommendation, investing is the only line item that has the highest cap. As you invest more of your money and you become a more skillful investor, you should get a larger return on your investments. Use that money very carefully and wisely. You might want to invest into your children's and grandchildren's education or business ventures. Like they say, *Give a man a fish and you feed him for a day. Teach a man to fish and you feed him for a lifetime.*

### 4)  Housing: Less than 25% of income

We have already talked about housing. Keep your housing payments lower than 25% of your income. "There's no place like home," truly … but make sure that the monthly cost is, at a maximum, 25% of your income. If you are above 25%, then I encourage you to make the necessary lifestyle changes to reduce it.

### 5)  Healthy Financials Improvements: Less than 20%

This is a line item I recommend to be less than 20%. Healthy financials improvements are the total amount of money that you will spend on improving your health and your finances. This is an important line item, because if you don't allocate the money to be spent on improvement, more than likely you will see it as a secondary item. Please refer to the two appendixes in the back of the book where you will find an expanded version of the following list with ideas and tools that can help you improve your health and your finances.

  ➢  Health improvements ideas:
  - Nutrition and natural foods
  - Chiropractic care
  - Stretching and exercising
  - Supplements
  - Body maintenance and tune up
  - Wellness classes

➢ Financial improvement ideas:
- Hire an accountant
- Hire a financial investment advisor
- Take financial investment classes
- Professional consulting
- Tax consulting
- Real estate investments classes

## 6) Education: Less than 15%

We are in a fast-pace era now. Business methods, systems, and processes are constantly changing. If you don't educate yourself, you will be "left behind." Go to school, buy books, take classes, seminars, audio books, DVDs—whatever form of education possible in order for you to be competitive in the marketplace.

# CHAPTER 8

# CONVERSATION WITH PROFESSIONALS

A couple of years ago while I was in the field selling medical software, I had the privilege of meeting Dr. Florence Foucauld, MD, Board Certified in Family Medicine. I have to say that she's one of the nicest people to talk to; she's friendly, kind, and amiable. When I told her I was writing a book on how to improve your health and finances, she was open to the idea and even found some time in her busy schedule to answer my questions.

### Throughout your practice, what are the biggest mistakes your patients make?

As a doctor it's important not only to consult my patients but also to give them the proper attention and time necessary in order to help them with whatever problems or situation they are facing.

The biggest mistake I see in some patients is that they come to me for the "magic pill". They expect a quick fix or a quick turnover to temporarily resolve their diseases. As you may know, a pill may in the short term, solve their problem; but understanding lifestyle changes should be a goal for their well being which will permanently solve their medical issues.

Most of my patients come to visit me for poor nutrition related topics. I get a lot of patients with chronic diseases such as obesity, high blood pressure and diabetes.

### In your years of experience as a doctor, what is the unforgettable client and story?

There was a patient of mine who was literally stuck in the past. When she was a kid she had been verbally abused by her parents and she couldn't move on with her life. All the negative words that were said by her parents, stayed with her while growing up. In the process she lost her self-esteem, confidence, and drive. Now she's obese and she's trying to lose weight. But until she crosses that mental barrier, until she makes peace with her childhood and seeks moral support from family members, she will not be able to move on and manage her weight properly.

**What are the two biggest suggestions that you recommend to your patients in order to improve their health?**

The number one suggestion to improve your health is restriction of calorie intake. People have a hard time with that, because they fail to acknowledge that as you get older, your body burns fewer calories. Therefore you need to adjust your eating habits and eat less as you get older. In the health field this is known as "Caloric Restriction":

My second suggestion is to find a way to manage stress properly. Stress is a killer. It affects your entire health and damages your body. Sleeping well, lifestyle changes, and exercising on a frequent basis are good ways to manage stress.

**Error! Hyperlink reference not valid.**
*Florence Foucauld, MD*
*Diplomat of American Board of Anti-aging & Regenerative Medicine*

Dr. Gustaveous Geiger is my chiropractor and a dear personal friend of mine and I can tell you that he has with a lot of experience and wisdom. When I have personal or health-related problems, I speak with him and he always has good answers. Not only is he a great doctor, but he's also a mentor filled with valuable experiences. When I mentioned to him that I would be writing a book, he was more than happy to help.

**Throughout your practice, what are the biggest mistakes your patients make?**

The biggest mistake I see all patients make is turning over responsibility for their health to the medical providers. Health care professionals can assist you in managing your health, but if you want to avoid being a victim of the health care system it is incumbent that you educate yourself about maintaining and sustaining your overall health. Our so called "health care system" is in fact a *sickness system* and they want to keep it that way. A system that thrives and relies on our ignorance. If I could snap my fingers and instantly we (including myself) were all disciplined to eat properly, get regular exercise and feed our minds with positive uplifting information, we would put *minimally 70%* of the doctors out of their traditional treatment patterns.

***In your years of experience as a doctor what is the unforgettable client and story?***

I don't have a singular amazing event that stands out in my mind, although there have been many special experiences. The most amazing event for me when adjusting a patient is when they realize that the body is a self-healing organism and it's capable of normalizing without the use of drugs. Now, please don't misinterpret what I am saying; there is a time and place for both drugs and surgery. But in our society, the driving force for both of those is not the patients overall health and well being. It's money. The big pharmaceutical companies run the show and anyone who dares get in their path, beware.

***What are the two biggest suggestions that you will recommend to your patients in order to improve their health.***

Consult with a competent alternative health and wellness provider, which includes many medical physicians. Take responsibility for your health by avoiding the *SAD* (Standard American Diet) of processed/fast foods, finding a reliable source for healthy food/ nutrition and committing to a regular exercise program. If you are not willing to do these things, you place yourself at the mercy of the *sickness care system* as we know it.

**Gustaveous Geiger, Jr., DC**
**Chiropractic Physician**

———— ❋ ————

Doctor Jacques Victor MD is my primary care physician and I believe that he is a great doctor. In my opinion, what makes Doctor Victor a great physician is his professionalism, honest opinion and medical advice when treating a patient. One of the reasons why he has been so successful in his practice is because he cares about his patients' health and well-being. Here's what Doctor Victor has to say:

### *Throughout your practice, what are the biggest mistakes your patients make?*

The biggest mistake I see in general throughout my practice is the misinformation and indiscriminate use of the internet. I want my patients to be well informed, but at the same time, I want them to take full advantage of office visits so that I can provide them with proper guidance, and to help dispel any doubts or confusion in a simple and accessible manner.

### *In your years of experience as a doctor, what is the unforgettable patient and story?*

During my medical practice covering more than 40 years, 2 medical cases come to mind as unforgettable.

While I was in the United States Air Force serving as a doctor, I was on call for the emergency room when suddenly I received a phone call from the doctor on duty. The doctor informed me that there was a baby that had been screaming all night long and starting to turn pale; my presence was required immediately, because they couldn't identify the problem. I rushed into the emergency room and asked the staff member if the total evaluation and complete workup had been done, to which they replied, yes. As I was in the consulting room looking at the baby, talking to the mom and trying to understand the situation, by instinct I removed the baby's diaper. Upon closer examination, my intuition was confirmed, the baby had a *strangulated hernia* (*a* strangulated hernia is a life threatening complication that *occurs when* blood flow to the hernia is cut off and the piece of tissue begins to die). The lesson to be learned from this story is, when you go see a physician:

1. Don't be in a rush, clearly explain your history and your condition.
2. Demand or allow the doctor do a thorough and in-depth evaluation of your condition.

From my experience listening to the patient and having a good patient history gives the doctor more than 50% chances of making a precise diagnosis and generating satisfactory results for patients.

The second story that I will never forget is that of an 11 year old boy who was in the emergency room the day before and was recommended to see a pediatrician the next day. The boy came to my Clinique because he wasn't feeling well. As I was getting ready to examine the boy, I noticed that he had long hair. Only when I pulled his hair back to take look at his ears did it become apparent that the boy had a deformity, he was missing the outer parts in both of his ears and had hearing aids. For me what was shocking was that the previous doctor's report completely omitted the fact that the boy had any type of anomaly in his ears, or that he had hearing aids.

The lesson to be learned in that story is the following:

1. If you are being referred to a specialist or another physician, make sure there is good communication between the two professionals regarding your condition and treatment; this way they can more accurately treat your condition.
2. Also even though the current physician treating you has notes from the previous physicians, he still needs to perform

his own physical examination instead of solely relying on the notes of the previous physician(s).

**What are the two biggest suggestions that you recommend to your patients in order to improve their health?**

In terms of improvement I can probably give a couple of important suggestions to improve your health:

1. Proper nutrition and hydration
2. Exercising
3. Mental health. Avoid stress by all means
4. Positive thinking: Deal with adversity the same way you deal with success

Juliette Morrow is my Pilates instructor at the gym that I attend. There are several Pilate's teachers at the gym but I think she's definitely one of the best for the following reasons:

1. During her intense one hour exercise routine, students stretch, sweat, strengthen and build core muscle.
2. Juliette pushes her students to the next level. Until this day, there are several exercises that I am able to start but not able to follow through, even though I am in good physical shape. I am still working hard to build up strength and stamina required to keep up with Juliette.
3. After classes, Juliette is always open to answer questions and help students achieve their desired fitness goals.

Juliette has been teaching Pilates, yoga, weight training, and cardiovascular exercises for twenty years and has taught physical fitness in the most prestigious gyms in New York and South Florida. During her career she has cultivated skills from a variety of trainers and with time and professional experiences; she has developed her own original movements for physical fitness.

When I told her about this book, she was totally committed to the idea of contributing with advice and encouragement. Here's what she has to say:

### *Throughout your career, what are the biggest mistakes your students make?*

The biggest mistake I see in my students is the way they breathe. The first and last thing you do in life is breathe, so getting it right is important. During my classes, I make a point to teach my students to exhale on the contraction exercises.

### *In your years of experience as an instructor, what is the unforgettable student and story?*

People attend my classes for different reasons, and as you can guess, one of those reasons is stress. I had a female student who was uptight and stressed out most of the time and unfortunately for me, one day I was 5 minutes late to teach a yoga class. This student berated and yelled at me in front of a class of 30 people. I calmly asked her to lie down and I started the class. Three weeks later, after some self-evaluation, she asked for my forgiveness; of course I forgave her.

### *What are the two biggest suggestions that you would recommend to your clients to improve their health?*

My number one advice is to eat a healthy, balanced diet, drink water, and get quality sleep. Secondly, I would encourage everyone to have a positive attitude about life; know that everything happens the way it is supposed to and we should be thankful for that.

Juliette Morrow, Certified Trainer
http://www.bodybeautifulbyjuliette.com/

———— ✳ ————

Patricia Hartman is a certified public accountant (CPA) and a partner in a firm where I do accounting and tax consulting on a part time basis. What I love about Patricia is her smile and her warm welcoming attitude. She is pleasant to work with; within one conversation you will notice her professionalism and her wealth of accounting and business expertise. Currently, most of her work focuses on forensic accounting, especially in divorce and fraud areas, but she is also an author and has written a few books. When I told her I was writing a book, not only did she give me some coaching and mentoring, but she gladly answered the following questions:

### *Throughout your practice, what are the biggest mistakes your clients make?*

One of the most costly mistakes I see business owners make is entering into partnerships, especially without agreements. Very few small business partnerships survive, because most partners have unstated expectations of the other. Commonly, one person has the money, the other the knowledge. Inevitably, one begrudges the other's efforts (or lack of) and believes they are doing it all or doing more. The 50/50 relationship is the worst, because it can be a stalemate on the business going forward. To compound the problem, owners often do not execute shareholder agreements or partnership agreements, so the expectations are not specified. Sometimes, one puts in money and the other blows through it, accomplishing nothing. Other times, one partner works hard to make the business a success, and is resentful of the other not doing anything, but getting half the profits.

### *In your years of experience as an accountant what is the unforgettable client and story?*

I remember being an accountant for a partnership and there was a disagreement between the two partners regarding the company expenses. The company tax return was originally filed by one of the partners and when the disagreement started, the other partner amended the tax return. When the first discovered this, he amended it yet again. They did not stipulate who was the authorized tax matters partner, and therefore, there was nothing either could do. Because they could not agree on what the business should be responsible for, they dissolved the corporation.

**What are the two biggest suggestions that you will recommend to your clients in order to improve their finances?**

I believe small business partnerships should be avoided, but if you are considering one, and if you are an entrepreneur, who needs capital, consider borrowing the money with some great terms (higher than market interest or a percentage of profit for a limited time). Be sure to hire a great attorney who does a lot of shareholder dispute work so they can help you negotiate an agreement that will be fair to both sides and will stipulate the expectations of each partner/shareholder which will reduce the resentment later.

**Patricia Coury Hartman, CPA/ABV/CFF, CFE, CVA**

Marc Heraux is my good friend and my personal business banker. He's actually a branch manager for the 5th *largest* retail bank in the US and he has been working in the banking industry for more than 15 years. Before having Marc as my financial banker, I never understood the real value added by having a knowledgeable banker. Throughout the years, I have learned to trust his counsel, and now every single financial decision I consider—whether related to his bank or not—I run it by him first to get his expertise and knowledge. Here's what Marc has to say:

### *Throughout your banking experience, what are the biggest mistakes your clients make?*

Most individuals don't understand the risk associated in their financial affairs. For instance:

- ➢ Cosigning for someone else on a loan: A co-signer will be liable almost as much as the original borrower.
- ➢ Identity theft: People who don't shred their statements or voided checks put themselves at risk.
- ➢ Having a will: The probate system can be expensive and exhausting. That's why it's extremely important to know the title and the names of the person on a bank account.

### *In your years of experience as a banker, what is the unforgettable client and story?*

I would say that out of a thousand clients that I know that are in debt only one client successfully managed to get out of debt and stay out of debt within one year's time. This guy was so determined and disciplined that he refinanced his house and took out some equity to pay some credit cards and car loan debt. He took a second job at night and on weekends, made several sacrifices in terms of spending habits and within only one year, he was out of debt. I will never forget that story because of the success rate ratio of 1/1000.

### *What are the two biggest suggestions that you will recommend to your clients to improve their finances?*

My first suggestion is to have a good banker as a trusted adviser who will help you:

- ➢ Assess risks
- ➢ Understand financial products
- ➢ Guide you through personal banking, business banking, investment banking, institutional banking, retail banking etc … My second suggestion is to read financial news in

order to be aware of changes, new technologies, new laws in place, new products or services available, and more. In addition, I will say that it's important to understand how life events will affect your finances. For example, how politics, the weather, and war can affect your finances.

# CHAPTER 9

# PLAN OF ACTION — HEALTH

Now that we reviewed the most important steps to improving your health and your finances, it's time to apply the Healthy Financials Formula PLEASE HELP methodology.

By now you must be wondering why this book is a First Edition? I would like you (the readers) to actively participate in the publishing of the second edition of the **Healthy Financials Formula: The Essential Guide to Improve Your True Personal Wealth.**

My goal is to help as many people as possible to improve their health and their finances.

Each reader has unique experiences when it comes to their health and finances, therefore I would like to gather "**the best**" elements (or principles) when it comes to the Healthy Financials Formula PLEASE HELP methodology by starting a conversation with the readers. I would like for each reader to share with me their philosophy, attitude, time management techniques, sources and resources etc….. that has been beneficial to them and also has affected their lives positively. I will gather the best elements and include them in the second edition of this book. Here is the best part of it: if our team chooses one of your elements you will receive the second edition of this book for free.

Please submit the following 8 items:

1. Name
2. Email address
3. Phone number (optional)
4. Mailing address
5. How did you hear about us
6. The principle(s) you would like to share with us:

### Philosophy
### Laws in place
### Estimate the cost

# Attitude
# Source and resources
# Effective time management

# Having a plan
# Evaluate
# Learn the fundamentals
# Practice disciplines

7.  A detail explanation why you think it's important
8.  Additional ideas or comments

Here is how you submit your information:

1.  Go to our website: www.healthyfinancials.com
2.  Click on the Contact tab
3.  Fill out the required field and submit your principle(s)

Or
Fax your information to:
(305) 224-1855

The examples I am about to share with you for this approach are only the beginning. As times goes by, you need to add to each element (or principle) and refine it in such a way that fits *you* best. In order to illustrate each point, I am giving you five examples for each principle starting with "health" and ending with "finance."

## PHILOSOPHY
- **Your Health Comes Before Your Finances**
People make this mistake all the time; they go to work and earn money, but neglect their health. Be cautious of that. Your health

comes before your finances. Not the other way around. I am sure if Steve Jobs and Bob Marley were alive today, they would completely agree with me. Both of them were multi-millionaires and passed away at a very young age due to illness.

- **A Sleeper Is a Winner**

  In general, your body needs rest to recover, typically about 7 to 8 hours per day. Allow me to share my story: I used to sleep 6 hours a day. During the day I would become fatigued and, in an effort to fight being so tired, I drank dark coffee for more energy. One day I read a book, *Health is Wealth*, (Health Value Publications, 2009) by Dr. Lou Ignaro. In it he wrote: *"Too often in our culture we make sleeplessness heroic, as though depriving ourselves of that which replenishes our bodies and mind is something to be proud of."* (Page 160) Since reading this, I now make it a priority to sleep a minimum of 7 hours a day ... and guess what? During the day I am full of energy and I don't need coffee to stay awake.

- **Healthy Lifestyle**

  I am an accountant and I spend most of my time behind a desk working. My chiropractor reminded me that the body is not designed for sitting behind a desk for long periods of time. No wonder I have back problems now. So I have learned: *balance your life!* The same way the body needs rest every day, it also needs *movement* every day.

- **Go Premium**

  There is an old saying that goes, "You are what you eat." When I go to the store for juice, I make sure not to get the "water and sugar" stuff. Instead, I buy a juice full of vitamins, antioxidants, and protein. Remember the acronym, "YOLO": You Only Live Once. So make sure you get the best food and drink that is affordable to you.

- **Sports Activities Are Not an Option**

Part of good health is to exercise at least 3 times a week. By exercising properly, you avoid a multitude of problems and restore your energy, focus, endurance, and strength.

## LAWS IN PLACE

Keep in mind, all of the following laws are already in place, and they will affect you whether you like it or not. My best advice is to learn them, and use them to your advantage.

- **Law of Sowing and Reaping**
  - ➤ Examples:
    - Do not expect to eat like crazy, become overweight, and still win a marathon.
    - Do not expect to play sports without the proper gear yet remain injury free.
    - Do not expect to eat very rapidly 10 ice cubes and be headache free.
  - ➤ **Well, then what about the following?**
    - How many people expect to be cancer free without taking daily antioxidants to help clean the cells in their body?
    - How many people who consume a lot of sugary stuff or items that convert into sugar expect to be diabetic free or heart disease free?
    - There is an old saying that goes like this: "Your outside is a pure reflection of what's going inside your mind and heart." Be careful of your thoughts, your intentions, and actions because more than likely they will come back to you with precise measure. There is an amazing book by Napoleon Hill called "Think and Grow Rich" that properly illustrate this idea of sowing and reaping

- **Law of Energy**

The body automatically produces energy, which eventually enables us to produce sound, movement, and heat. I remember learning in high school physics that energy cannot be created or destroyed, only converted from one form to another (Albert Einstein). How does that apply to us? How long does it take to stay around negative, critical, and complaining people before you become negative, critical and a complainer?

- **Law of Life**

Every living creature is born and, one day, will die. If you are alive, death is inevitable.

In that middle section—Life and Time—we can play a major and active role. One way to extend this period, and to resist death is to engage in activities that nourish the body, restore health and delay the aging process.

- **Law of Alignment/Balance**

Have you ever gone to the chiropractor for a chiropractic adjustment? Earlier this week, I went to my chiropractor and I didn't even know that I was misaligned until he showed me. All your nerves are connected to your spine, and, therefore, a chiropractic adjustment:

➢ Improves respiration
➢ Improves range of motion
➢ Improves heart rate variability and autonomic function
➢ Improves cardiovascular functions
➢ Improves muscle strength
➢ And much more

Christians believe that humans are a triune being composed of:

1. Physiological: The Body
   - Smell
   - HearingTaste
   - Touch
   - Sight

2. Spiritual: The Spirit
   - Intuition
   - Conscience
   - Communication

3. The Soul
   - Mind
   - Emotions
   - Will

When those three areas are in alignment, not only do you honor God, but you also increase your fellowship with Him as well.

- **Law of Interdependence**
  The definition of the Law of Interdependence is the relation between two different kinds of organisms in which one benefits from the other.

  Why is that important for you to know? The answer is simple: to avoid negligence in certain areas of your health. Did you know: If your heart doesn't pump enough blood to your brain, you can have a stroke.
  - If your heart doesn't function properly, you can become out of breath.
  - If your digestive system is unclean or clogs up, it affects your energy level and your skin.

➢ If your liver is unclean, it will affect your heart and almost every organ in your body.

Earlier, we spoke about the body, spirit, and the soul. In my opinion, not only do they need to be in alignment, but they are interdependent on each other as well.

In the Bible the book of Matthew reads: *"It is written: 'Man shall not live on bread alone, but on every word that comes from the mouth of God'"* (Matthew 4:4 NIV). In other words, in order to live well, not only do we need bread to feed our body, we also need the words of God to feed our mind, soul, and spirit.

## ESTIMATE THE COST

I am pretty sure that at some point in your life, you had to calculate the cost of something. As an accountant, I can tell you there are several types of cost.

But, let's see how the cost factor applies to your health:

- **Monetary Cost**
  The definition is fairly straightforward: The monetary cost is an amount that has to be paid or given up in order to get something. I face that decision every week when I go to the grocery store; should I buy organic apples or regular apples. The majority of the time I pay more for the organic apples (which goes back to the philosophy of Going Premium.)

- **Opportunity Cost**
  The definition is fairly straightforward as well. The cost of an alternative that must be forgone in order to pursue a certain action. In other words, the benefits you could have received by taking an alternative action. Let's say you've been performing well at your job or your business and a client or boss or partner decides to take you to a fancy restaurant to celebrate. But that same day is your "fasting day" because of the following benefits:

> ➤ Fasting detoxifies your body.
> ➤ Fasting increases breakdown of glucose; this way, the body creates more energy.
> ➤ Fasting builds immunity to cancer and other diseases.
> ➤ Fasting promotes resolution of inflammatory diseases and allergies. Examples of such inflammatory diseases are rheumatoid arthritis, arthritis, and skin diseases such as psoriasis.

Let's say you end up declining that invitation, here is your opportunity cost:

> ➤ The opportunity to get out of the office and do something nice.
> ➤ The opportunity to get a free lunch.
> ➤ Not only the opportunity for a free meal, but a nice free meal with appetizer, entrée, dessert, and perhaps a nice glass of wine or a cocktail. (Right now, I'm thinking of warm brown wheat bread with olive oil and soy sauce, followed by shrimp cocktail, potatoes and asparagus, and cheesecake with strawberries ...)

*Wow.* That's a difficult choice.

- **Short-term Cost**

Let's say every morning you drink an antioxidant tea to help cleanse the cells in your body. The short-term cost you have to pay is that you must drink a bitter tea, taking time to drink it every day. But, in the end, that's smart because it means you are thinking about your present and future health.

- **Long-term Cost**

This is the opposite of short-term cost. Let's say weeks and months pass by and you don't take any antioxidants or vitamins. The long term cost is the following:

  ➢ Pain
  ➢ Robs you of the enjoyment of life
  ➢ Destroys your marvelous body
  ➢ Increases your chances of premature death

- **Direct and Indirect Cost**

In order to have and to maintain good health, generally speaking, we have two choices:

  ➢ Prevention: Indirect costs. Eating healthy foods and taking supplements not only provides you with some immediate health benefits, but it increases your overall health and chances of avoiding long-term complications. This is an indirect cost of good health.
  ➢ Health Problems: Direct cost. When you are sick and you have to constantly go to the doctor and take expensive medication, even sometimes undergo surgery, that's a direct health cost.

## ATTITUDE

I believe that attitude can be one of your greatest assets, but at the same time, if you don't manage it properly, it can become your greatest liability. Your attitude toward information, people, society, events, etc. totally depends on you. For the most part, this is something you have control of.

I find that the following attitudes toward your health can lead to some amazing results: **Get Serious** When it comes to your health, you have to be very *serious*. Understand that without proper health, you may have a bank account with millions of dollars, but you will still be poor. Your body needs to be maintained and nourished in order for you to fulfill your dreams. This is crucial.

- **Be Proactive**

   You have to be proactive with your health. If you are sick, go see a doctor. If you have an illness, get a book and learn about it. If you are a little bit overweight, go to the gym. It's important that you take action if something is not functioning properly.

- **Be Willing to Go the Extra Mile**

   Does this ever happen to you: After a long day of work, your body is all cranked up, you are tired, your mind is telling you to go home and go to bed, but deep down inside you know that you have to go to the gym and/or exercise. Going the extra mile is always worth it. It is the difference between "okay" health and "good" health.

- **Be Cautious**

   There are so many products out there, it's hard to know which one is good. On the flip side, there is so much information out there, you don't know what or whom to believe. Here is the best advice I can give you: read, listen, study, or review different types of information but make sure your final decision is based upon your own conclusion, not what someone else tells you.

- **Be a Good Student**

   I personally believe everyone should be a student of good health. In order to have good health, there is so much to learn. Here's a quick list:

   ➢ Nutrition
   ➢ Anti-Aging
   ➢ Digestion
   ➢ Stretching

➤ Vegetables

➤ Fruits

➤ Types of Physicians to Visit

➤ Disease Prevention

➤ Body Fat

➤ Muscles, etc.… To me, having good health is a lifetime study that never ends.

## SOURCES AND RESOURCES

The other day, I was browsing the news and read about a major company that was being sued because of false advertising. They had been claiming that their yogurts were "clinically" and "scientifically" proven to regulate digestion and boost the immune system. That company finally settled the lawsuit, but it cost them millions.

My friend, your sources and resources are important. I cannot emphasize enough how important this is. For example, let's say a friend of yours (a source) tells you that taking Coq10 helps with your energy level and helps reduce heart failure. How do you validate that info? Perhaps you have a good book in your home library that talks about that very subject. Or, you find a reliable website. Or, better still, you know a doctor who is an expert on that subject and he/she can confirm that statement (resources).

Here is a good list of sources & resources:

• **Referral**

Word of mouth is still one of the best ways of discovering good services and products. If one of your friends, family members, or coworkers is getting some good results, ask them for the name of that source.

• **Biblical**

In my opinion the Bible is by far one of the greatest books known to mankind. And the reality is that it covers almost every subject needed in order to be healthy, successful, powerful, and unique.

Go to your library and look in the nutrition or diet section. You will be amazed at how many books talk about fruits and vegetables and how they are good for your health. Then, look in the Bible, specifically in (Daniel 1: 11-15 NIV) where it says, *"Please test your servants for ten days: Give us nothing but vegetables to eat and water to drink. Then compare our appearance with that of the young men who eat the royal food, and treat your servants in accordance with what you see." So the king's guard agreed to this and tested them for ten days. At the end of the ten days, they looked healthier and better nourished than any of the young men who ate the royal food."*

- **Associations**

Associations are a great source of information. Usually if there is a demand, professionals will assemble and create an association. There are associations for cancer, diabetes, the heart, etc.

- **Studies**

Universities can be a great source of information. Not only do they have libraries and bookstores, but they have professors who may be willing to talk to you about their research or share information. Harvard Medical School has a great newsletter and a special health report.

- **Libraries**

If you haven't been to a library in a while, you might be surprised to see the information they currently possess. For example, when I had my back problem, I was able to go to the library where I found some great books and DVD's talking about lower back pain.

## EFFECTIVE TIME MANAGEMENT

All of us have the same amount of time during the day—24 hours. Depending on your activity level, you can have enough time to take care of your health, or you don't have the time. My recommendation is to find the necessary time to take care of yourself. Here is a good list of the activities that should be in your weekly schedule.

> ➤ Sleeping time (You should sleep a minimum of 7 to 8 hours per day.)
> ➤ Exercise Time (You should exercise at least 4 times during the week.)
> ➤ Prayer & Meditation (Daily prayer and meditation keeps you grounded and focused.)
> ➤ Nutrition (Take your time when you eat. Chew your food well; it's good for your digestion.)
> ➤ Repair and Maintenance (Your body requires maintenance. A few examples of maintaining your body is massage, annual physicals, chiropractic adjustments, Detox, fasting, and staying "up" on the latest health information.

## HAVE A PLAN

There is an old saying that goes: "Failing to plan, is planning to fail." In other words, if you fail to make a plan, that means you made a decision either consciously or unconsciously to participate in your failure. There is a big difference between having your day planned before it starts and "taking the day as it comes." Some plans that may be included in your day are:

• **Nutrition Plan**

Whether you are following the 6-1 method or the 5-2 method, for your days of healthy eating you need to first be prepared. You should know the fruits and vegetables that are beneficial to your health. You should know what to purchase at the grocery store and the types of restaurants to avoid or visit.

• **Exercise plan**

Your body is not composed of only bones and muscles. You have organs, ligaments, the immune system, etc. Therefore, it's unlikely that you will exercise your entire body in one day. It's important to have a schedule. For example two times a week for cardio, 1 day a week for strength training and weight lifting, one day for yoga and stretching.

- **Lifestyle Plan (Balance)**

  Something happened to me this month and it's kind of hard to believe. I don't have a full explanation of why it happened but I've noticed the results and I'm enjoying them.

  Before my back issue, I used to work at least 10 hours a day, 6 days a week and exercise once or twice a week. I spent most of my time in an office sitting behind the computer. About 3 months ago, I started to have back problems. I decided to find a solution to my problems with a vengeance. As a result, I made the following lifestyle changes:

  - ➢ I reduced my office hours.
  - ➢ I exercise *every day* for at least 20 minutes (at home or at the gym).
  - ➢ I take yoga classes (for breathing and stretching).
  - ➢ I am eating healthier, including eating more organic foods.
  - ➢ I go swimming at least once a week.
  - ➢ From time to time, I go to the sauna and Jacuzzi.

  Well, guess what happened. First I should tell you that in recent years I have been going bald. Quickly. Yet now, for some reason I am seeing more hair on my head. Interesting. From this I have learned that being unbalanced doesn't lead to anywhere good. Balancing your life can not only help restore health in the areas you desire, but also in other areas you didn't initially thought of as well. Balancing your life covers a *multitude* of health aspects.

- **Sleeping plan**

  We have already talked about this. Getting enough sleep is not an option; your body needs at least 7 to 8 hours per day of rest in order to function properly.

- **Prevention Plan**

A prevention plan is crucial. Taking supplements, eating properly, stretching or exercising every day is something that, if you are not already doing so, you should start and continue. Please check our website www.healthyfinancials.com for upcoming products and services.

## EVALUATE

Whenever you have systems in place, you need to evaluate whether they are working or not. Or, perhaps you need to implement a couple of activities in order to fix whatever you are currently doing.

- **Blood Tests**

Doing yearly blood tests along with your annual checkup can reveal a lot of things regarding your current health condition such as deficiencies or excess in your nutritional intake. For example, until I had a recent blood test, I was unaware that I was deficient in vitamin B12.

- **Blood pressure**

Whether you suffer from hypertension (high blood pressure) or hypotension (low blood pressure), it's a great idea to keep a check on it at interval times. You can have a blood pressure monitor (sphygmomanometer) at home or go to the nearest pharmacy or doctor's office to check how your heart's "engine" is doing.

- **Weight**

Check your weight at least once every three months. Being overweight can lead to serious complications. Whether you are on an exercise and nutritional plan or not, check your weight to monitor the results.

- **Annual checkup**

Have you ever been to the dentist and been told that you have a cavity that you weren't aware of? A yearly checkup can actually prevent disastrous results such as losing your permanent teeth and/or the expense of dental surgery, root canals, crowns, bridges, etc.

- **Personal notes**

This might be new to you, but it's a good idea to monitor yourself. Let's say you have a personal journal or food journal. You can write how you feel after you eat or drink something. In my journal I recently wrote how I felt after eating red meat. I didn't sleep well that evening. Recording it helps me to remember in order not to make the same mistake again. Now if I do eat red meat, I know and understand the cost.

## LEARN THE FUNDAMENTALS

I believe that having good health is learning the fundamentals of what good health entails. Anyone can have their own opinion and preferences. That doesn't make them right or wrong. Being in good health is a combination of healthy practices, and knowing and properly applying the fundamentals.

I went to a seminar where the presenting doctor was convinced that nitric oxide supplementation was part of the fundamentals of good health. One benefit being that it widens your arteries and veins for better circulation of blood, which in turn helps prevent heart disease. More than likely, the doctor is right. But since I don't have a medical background, the following list will reflect more on the nutritional aspects of good health. I truly believe it's a quest and an obligation to our health to find out the fundamentals of good health.

- **Cellular Nutrition**

It's crucial to know that the body is made up of at least 5 billion cells. From your heart to your liver, from your reproductive system to your digestive systems, all of them are made of cells. Once you understand what your cells need and don't need to function properly, you can revolutionize your health. You can see an increase in energy, avoid cancer, slow the process of aging, prevent heart disease, and so much more.

- **Hydration**

  Our body is composed of 60-70 % percent water. You may not see it or feel it, but it's true. So what do you do with that information? For one, drink more water every day. Drinking water is like renewing your body. In the Book *Discover Wellness: How Staying Healthy Can Make You Rich by Bob Hoffman and Jason Deitch*, a doctor describes it as buying insurance, because it helps you avoid so many health complications. When you drink a lot of water, not only do you quench your thirst, but it also helps you eliminate toxins.

- **Prayer & Meditation**

  Earlier we talked about meditation and prayer. You can feed your body and take care of yourself with the best in terms of products, services, and food. This doesn't mean that you will be fully healthy. Remember, humans are not composed of flesh only. We have the body, the spirit, and the soul. Daily prayer and meditation is a must. They improve your mood, reduce high blood pressure and stress, and help you stay focused and happy.

- **Movement**

  If you talk to a medical doctor or a physical therapist, they will tell you that exercise is a must for good health. We've already discussed this, but allow me to remind you that:

  - ➤ Strength exercise helps increase your power and boost metabolic rate.
  - ➤ Exercise helps increase oxygen intake.
  - ➤ Exercise and flexibility training help increase range of motions and posture.

If you talk to a pastor, he will tell you the body was made for movement. In Genesis, we read that God created man, and then afterward, He created a garden. Then, check out what God did—*The Lord God took the man and put him in the Garden of Eden to work it and keep it* (Genesis 2:15 NIV). God did not put man in the garden to look at it, but to *move within it and take care of it.*

- **Chemical Balance**

Earlier we spoke about activity balance, now we need to talk about chemical balance. Throughout the human body we have several chemical reactions and mechanisms. Once the system is out of balance, we start incurring some problems. Two examples of chemical imbalance are:

- Insulin imbalance

Insulin is a hormone produced by the pancreas that opens up microscopic pathways and allows glucose, or sugar, to enter the cells. At normal levels, enough insulin is produced and used by the body to allow adequate glucose to be absorbed by the cells for energy purposes. If there is an imbalance of insulin you run the risk of becoming diabetic.

- Metabolic imbalance

Your metabolic system is composed of chemical reactions that directly affect your energy, appetite, and weight. If your metabolic system is not in balance, you run the risk of having diseases related to weight control.

## PRACTICE DISCIPLINES

Practice disciplines are the equivalent of repetition, repetition, repetition. For example, the discipline of eating healthy 6 days is so effective and powerful only to the degree of you spending the entire 6 days eating healthy. Not two days or three days of eating healthy.

*Discipline* is really the "secret sauce" for good health. It's hard to be consistent, but that's where your treasures are.

Michael Jordan is undoubtedly one of the best basketball players off all time, and Rodger Federer is one of the best tennis players of all time as well, but they didn't become great athletes overnight. Like them, you must have a good set of disciplines. Here is a good list:

➤ Eat healthy and exercise regularly
➤ Hydrate, hydrate, hydrate
➤ Spend time daily in meditation and prayer
➤ Sleep at least 7-8 hours per day
➤ Supplement your diet with vitamins and other supplements that your body requires.

# CHAPTER 10

# PLAN OF ACTION — FINANCES

This morning, on my way to work, I saw a guy driving his car *and* brushing his teeth at the same time. Wow. Are you serious? While it's legally permissible, how *smart* is it? The same can be said of your finances. There are a thousand different ways to go about managing your finances, but my hope for you is that you find the proper formula that fits *you* best so that you can be successful with your finances. Let's jump back in the discussion of finances with our Healthy Financials Formula PLEASE HELP acronym methodology.

## PHILOSOPHY

- **Bring Value**

This might be simplistic, but it's essential to know: you must bring value to the market place. In other words, solve a problem, help someone, and/or bring seed to the soil in order for it to grow. I do this constantly. Clients bring me their bank statements, I do the bookkeeping for them, issue their financials, and then translate and summarize their activities into numbers for better management decisions.

- **Mind Your Own Business**

The United States government gives big tax breaks to business owners. Not only does managing your own business help save money in taxes, but the owner has the chance to control their own destiny. There is no cap to your income potential. There's also little limit to the number of hours you can work, so be careful there. I first discover this philosophy by reading a very good book called *"Rich Dad Poor Dad" by Robert Kiyosaki.* He does a great job at explaining how minding your business can change your life.

- **Service to Many Leads to Fortune**

In the Bible we find in the book of Mark *"Anyone who wants to be first, must be the very last, and the servant of all"* (Mark 9:35 NIV).

Jim Rhon, American entrepreneur, author, and motivational speaker has a saying, "Find a way to serve the many, for service to many leads to greatness for those that are interested."

Bill Gates, one of the richest people in the world, is a famous example of this principle. The company he created, Microsoft, has more than 80% market share of operating system software in the world. Is it any wonder why he is a multi-billionaire?

- **Team Player**

If you think you are going to do something great in this world by yourself, good luck. Team effort is the way to achieve great things. Look at the highest example. God himself, when He created the world, said, *"Let us make mankind in our image, in our likeness"* (Genesis 1:26 NIV). When Jesus walked upon the earth, His ministry was composed not of himself alone, but of 12 disciples and when He sent them out on active duty, He sent them out by twos.

Google, Inc. is the biggest internet search engine in the world, and it wasn't founded alone. Sergey Brin, Larry Page, and Eric Schmidt all had a hand in it.

While Disney Land and Disney World were the "brain child" of Walt Disney, he was not alone in the creation of the theme parks.

Charlie Munger and Warren Buffet worked together to grow Berkshire Hathaway, the American multinational conglomerate investment company.

I would be negligent if I didn't mention that 90% of the people in the world won't match your style, work ethics, attitudes, and values. Therefore be careful of whom you associate with.

- **Investor**

To do well financially, you have to be an investor. Whether you invest with your money, time, resources, or talents, you have to be willing to put something on the table and you have to be willing to give up some things in order to get more. But it's not enough to just be an investor; you also need to be a *smart* investor. Smart investors calculate and monitor their return on investments. (ROI)

## LAWS IN PLACE

- **Sowing and Reaping**

  We have already discussed this in a previous chapter, so I won't go into too much detail. But one point I will address—how are you sowing your time? Are you spending your time creating products or services for one person or thousands of people? There is a big financial difference in the end results of those two paths.

- **Compounding Interest**

  Let's not forget the law of compounding interest. It's a very powerful force. If you invest $15,000 at 12% annual interest and contribute $150/ month to an investment plan for 30 years, it will give $1,068,731. Meanwhile only $69,000 came out of your pocket. Now that's awesome.

- **Law of Inflation**

  A one dollar bill in today's market will be worth less five years from now. In economics, inflation is the rise in the general level of prices of goods and services in an economy over a period of time. This really matters in terms of investment because sometimes you have to know if you should keep your money in cash or allocate it toward different kinds of assets.

- **Law of Attraction**

  You will attract the thoughts or ideas you allow to dominate your mind. In other words "like attracts like." A couple of years ago there was a great documentary called *"The Secret" by Rhonda Byrne* which illustrate this point very clearly. Why is that important in the finance section? It's simple: Are you mostly thinking how to spend money or make money?

- **Law of Focus**

I have also mentioned this law previously. The law of focus states that "the more you stay focused, the better your odds of succeeding." In order to win financially, you have to stay focused. There are so many distractions and income producing activities that if you do not stay centered on a few activities you know how to do well, you will more than likely miss out on your potential.

Also, if you don't monitor and focus on your net worth, how do you expect it to increase? **ESTIMATE COST**

- **Monetary Cost**

We covered this definition in the previous chapter. Whatever you are going to purchase has a cost attached to it, so make sure you can afford it. A good example of looking to the future as well as the present is to remember what happened with the housing bubble in the US, 2006-2009. Many people were purchasing houses they couldn't afford and, in the end, we were left with a massive foreclosure epidemic.

- **Investment Cost**

Investment cost is simply the cost to participate in an investment venture. Be very careful about this type of cost. For example, when it comes to mutual funds, make sure you know the cost associated with them. Or, if you have to buy your way into a business, keep in mind the accounting fees, business evaluations, consulting fees, etc.

- **Opportunity Cost**

We previously mentioned the definition of opportunity cost. For example, these days a lot of young professionals who are getting their Masters Degree are analyzing this type of cost. "Should I not work for three years to go to law school?" Or "Should I forgo $210,000 in wages to pursue an education?"

- **Fixed Cost/Variable Cost**

Fixed costs are business expenses that are not dependent on the level of goods or services produced by the business. A good example is the rent or lease you pay for an office, etc. This is usually considered a "fixed" cost. Variable costs are expenses that change in proportion to the activity of a business. A good example of this variable cost is merchant services. The higher you charge a client, the more fees you will pay to the merchant services company.

- **Differential Cost**

Differential cost is a business term that refers to the difference in costs for a business when choosing between two alternatives. For example, should I invest my money myself or should I give it to an institution to invest for me?

## ATTITUDE

- **Be a Student**

The financial market place is very complex nowadays. Mutual funds, retirement accounts, taxes, stocks, options, bonds, credit reports and scores, the Security Exchange and Commission (SEC), annuities, tax differed accounts, rollovers … There is no way on earth you will know everything. Therefore, always be a student.

- **Ready to Work (Serve)**

In the Bible in the book of Proverb we read: *Lazy hands make a man poor, but diligent hands bring wealth* (Proverb 10:4 NIV). Always have that attitude to be ready for service in whatever capacity you can. Do not be lazy. Discover what your talents are and explore them. That's why I believe each person should have their own business, whether part time or full time.

- **Be Eager to Earn Rather than Spend**

In general, it's easier to spend money than it is to make it. But just as the opportunities are vast to spend money, so are the opportunities to make money. Look around you at people's needs. What do you have that you could offer in the way of services or products that would fill those needs?

- **Visionary**

Remember that each minute that passes holds a chance for us to make a difference in order to have a better future. But first you must imagine a better future. All of it begins in your mind. Imagine looking at your personal financial statement and it shows passive income coming in every month. Or imagine yourself having an excessive amount of cash, and now your responsibility is to allocate it properly.

- **Bold**

Being bold can make a significant difference in your paycheck. Use your mouth to speak, be courageous, ask tough questions, write lucrative contracts, make low discount offers, show up at unexpected meetings, raise your voice at opportune times to make a point, etc.

## SOURCES AND RESOURCES

With so much information out there, it's hard to know what to believe. We are living in a society where information has truly become power. With technology and the internet, information is being spread at a faster speed than ever. Be careful who you trust and believe. Everything I have written in this book should be both questioned and verified. I believe I have told you the truth, but do your due diligence and test the principles for yourself.

- **Networks**

The other day I heard a sermon from my home church in which one of the assistant pastor talked about the law of exposure. He said that everything we know, talk about, or think is because we've been exposed to it. And it's true. Later on, my pastor Mike Patz from

Greenhouse Church re-elaborated that point to some degree by saying that we are "voice activated."

> ➤ We don't give what we don't possess.
> ➤ We don't share what we don't know.
> ➤ We don't express what we don't feel.

Why am I saying all of this? Be very, very careful who you hang out with. Because your family, friends, and coworkers will rub their traits off on you—consciously or unconsciously. If your close friends are broke, guess what? You will probably end up being broke as well. There is an old saying that goes like this *"your income is the average of your 5 closest friends"*

- **Read reports**
Start with your own personal financial statement. Read it. A lot of people don't know how they are doing financially. Look at a company's financials. Go on the internet to read charts and prospectus reports. You don't have to have a master in all fields, but take your time to read some financial reports.

- **Books & Periodicals**
You probably already know this, but I will reemphasize it again. Not all information being put out there by the media is good information. Buy books, regarding financials, read what wiser people have to say regarding the subject you are interested in. Your local public library is a treasure. Bookstores and online bookstores such as Amazon.com and Goodreads.com are awesome places to find books.

- **Mentoring**
If you can find a great mentor to share with you his successes and failures, it will serve you wonderfully. That person can share with you a business formula that works and also tell you what traps

to avoid. But even though having a mentor can be a good thing, be careful not to make that person an idol.

- **Cash**

Your money is a personal resource. This might sound redundant, simplistic, and useless ... but it's profound. You can either use your money to purchase dessert or a cup of coffee or piece of costume jewelry. Or, you can use it to purchase a book that tells you more about finance. You can either use your money to invest or to spend. Your choices will most probably be based on your maturity and experiences in life.

## EFFECTIVE TIME MANAGEMENT

We all possess the same number of hours in a day and we have to know how to best manage that time. When it comes to finance, I believe the following 5 areas will help with this principle:

- **Active/Passive Income**

It's impossible to be financially independent if you spend all your time working for wages. My simple suggestion is that you start creating passive income as soon as possible and then spend more time creating and improving those sources of income instead of *working* for your wages for the rest of your life.

- **Read, Read, Read**

People who succeed financially spend time reading—good sources with good information. I recently saw a documentary about Warren Buffet, in which his wife shared how fed up she had become with him because he spent so much time reading. This should give you a clue as to why he's one of the richest people in the world.

- **Plan Your Day Ahead**

What I am about to say is so powerful: prepare your day before it starts. This way you will go into the day focused and determined to finish what you had originally planned. Life has so many distractions (phone calls, internet, social media, friends, family, computer issues); if you allow them to take over, you will never accomplish what you truly want to do with your life.

- **Six to One Ratio**

    When I discovered this principle in the Old Testament of the Bible, it completely changed my life. According to the Word of the Lord, we are to have six days of work and one day of rest. Before knowing this principle I used to feel guilty about taking so much as a nap on weekends. Not anymore. I can tell you that if you put the practice of working six days and resting one, it works. I actually found that I make more money by following the six to one principle instead of working every day.

- **Delegation**

    Remember, you only have 24 hours during the day; you have to delegate certain tasks. I see this all the time with small business owners, even with myself when I first started in business. I used to spend time designing my own business cards and brochures. I don't do that anymore; I pay someone else to do it for me. Here is why:

    ➢ I can use that time to produce more income.
    ➢ I don't have the skills and expertise to do it both properly and professionally.
    ➢ I lack the tools (software) for the professional look.

## HAVE A PLAN

- Passive Income Plan

    I have often mentioned passive income. It's important for your financial security that you start creating a passive income plan. Here are a few ideas:

- ➢ Rental real estate
- ➢ Licensing software
- ➢ Have people working for you
- ➢ Stock portfolio investment
- ➢ Income-generating website
- ➢ Network marketing
- ➢ Retirement Plan

In the section titled "Budget," I mentioned investing at least 10% of your income for retirement purposes. I must add this: be *extremely* careful who manages your money. Remember what happened with the Enron employees? They lost everything in their company pension plan.

- **Debt Free Plan**

  Get out of debt as soon as possible. This way the money you currently use to pay your debts, you can use to increase your investments and hopefully get a greater Return on Investment (ROI).

- **Financially Independent Plan**

  Financially independent means that you have your money working *for* you and your money is generating enough yearly income that you don't have to work in order to live well.

- **Tax Reduction Plan**

  I have to mention this. Did you know there are several type of taxes? A few examples are:

  - ➢ Income tax
  - ➢ Gift tax
  - ➢ Real estate tax
  - ➢ Capital gain tax
  - ➢ Estate tax

If you want to succeed financially, you need to have a tax reduction plan. There are several ways to reduce your taxes. In our company Healthy Financials Inc we can help you come up with a tax reduction plan depending on your circumstances.

## EVALUATE

- **Ratio Study**

Start with your own financials by evaluating your ratio percentages. Are you spending too much on food? Are you spending too much on your housing payment? Are your debt payments too high?

- **Financial Review**

A quarterly financial review is not a bad idea. Sit down with your accountant or financial adviser and see how you can improve your numbers. Again, it's *crucial* for *you* to review your financials. At Healthy Financials Inc we have an excellent service called "Financial TuneUp" which is an accounting service that will allow you to properly assess and monitor your finances in order to grow and prosper financially. A financial review can reveal several things such as:

a) Unknown expenses
b) Percentage of expenses as a line item. For example a lot of times when I do a financial review for my clients they are surprised at how much money they spend on food
c) Net operating loss. (You are in the red)
d) Profit margin
e) And much more

- **Class Evaluation**

On the website of the financial company that I invest my money with, they show an asset class allocation of people with the same age as me. It's not a bad idea to compare yourself with others. It can give you the motivation to do better.

- **Settle Accounts**

If you are a manager or someone responsible for overseeing others, make sure you review the work of those you are managing. In the accounting world, we have review layers: The bookkeeper does the work, the accountant reviews it and the owner of the business reviews it one last time before submitting it to the client. At the end of the day, the business *owner* is responsible for the quality of the work.

- **Budgeted/Actual Report**

Let's say in the beginning of 2012 you said that your goal for the year was to make $100,000, of which you planned to invest at least $20,000. How did you do? I hope in the beginning of each year you will look at your numbers from the previous year to see how you performed. This way you will take note of necessary changes in order to do better in the future.

## LEARN THE FUNDAMENTALS

- **Personal Financial Statement**

I have already talked a lot about this in previous chapters so I will only say this—one of the *fundamentals* in finance is your personal financial statements.

- **Budget**

I have already spoken of this in detail as well, but it bears repeating: a budget is *fundamental* in finance.

- **Interest**

Whether it's the interest rate you pay on your mortgage or the interest you receive on a CD (Certificate of Deposit or Certificate of

Death) account in the bank, interest matters. Check out this house mortgage example:

Loan Term Fixed: 30 Years
Interest rate: 5.5 %
Amount borrowed: $300,000
**Result**: Total Payments: $613,212.12
**Result:** Total interest paid: $313,212.12
(At this rate, you will pay more interest
than the price of the house itself.)

- **Investments**

Investments are part of the fundamentals of finance. It's important to fully know and understand your long-term and short-term investment plans.

- **Planning**

Planning might not sound like a fundamental in finance, but it is. Here are couple of things you need to consider in planning your finances:

- ➢ Housing
- ➢ Retirement
- ➢ Insurance
- ➢ Asset allocation and classification
- ➢ Education
- ➢ Estate
- ➢ Taxes

## PRACTICE DISCIPLINE

- **Live on Less than You Make**

This is an easy principle to adopt. Just *live on less money than you make*. That's how people *with* money, *have* money.

- **Monitor Your Net Worth.**
  I cannot emphasize enough how important this is. Take at least 30 minutes a month and "just do it."

- **Read, Read, and Read**
  I've said this before but I'll say it again: read new material pertaining to your industry or line of work in order to get better. Read as much as you can about financial success strategies.

- **Review**
  You need to review your performance and/or the performance of your team on a periodic basis. This is how you grow.

- **Improvement**
  There is always room for improvement. Improve the following, which ultimately will improve your income if you put it to work:

  ➢ Vocabulary
  ➢ Skills
  ➢ Systems and processes
  ➢ Persuasion methods
  ➢ Charisma

*Tony Robbins* wrote an amazing book called *"Awaken a giant within"* that has a simple and very effective formula for improvement by the name of CANI. Constant and never-ending improvement. Therefore please keep improvement on your schedule.

# CHAPTER 11

# CONCLUSION

I hope you have enjoyed the content of this book, and most importantly that you will test the ideas I've shared with you to see if they work. I believe this book should be the beginning of your journey to improve your health and your finances. You should read many other books to be healthy and wealthy, listen to audio tapes and attend seminars in order to improve your health and your finances. But while you are on your quest to improvement, keep in mind the PLEASE HELP formula. I believe it's a great foundation you can build upon.

- **Philosophy**
- **Laws in Place**
- **Estimate Cost**
- **Attitude**
- **Source and Resources**
- **Effective Time Management**
- **Have a Plan**
- **Evaluate**
- **Learn the Fundamentals**
- **Practice Disciplines**

My entire reason for writing this book can be summed up in the following story. When I read this story, it brought me so much hope I felt I had to share it.

But before I do share this story with you, I would like to reveal to you one of the biggest secrets I learned in the last two years. Learning this secret completely changed my life and habits for my better future. Here is the secret:

"GOD IS CONDITIONAL"

What do I mean, you ask?

In the Bible we read the following:

*Come near to God and he will come near to you* (James 4:8 NIV).

*Draw near to God and He will draw near to you* (James 4:8 NKJ).

From this scripture, we understand that the more time we spend having a personal relationship with God, the more He will manifest in our lives. In other words, the more time you spend praying, reading the Bible, and doing God's will, the more He will manifest and create miracles in our lives. For instance, God's will is for us to improve ourselves and become better human beings in order for us to enjoy life to its fullest. We read the following in the scriptures:

> *"The Lord is not slow in keeping his promise, as some understand slowness. Instead he is patient with you, not wanting anyone to perish"* (2 Peter 3:9 NIV).

> *""For I know the plans I have for you," declares the LORD, "PLANS TO PROSPER you and not to harm you, plans to give you hope and a future""* (Jeremiah 29:11 NIV).

> *"Command those who are rich in this present world not to be arrogant nor to put their hope in wealth, which is so uncertain, but to put their hope in God, who richly provides us with everything for our enjoyment"* (1 Timothy 6:17 NIV).

For instance, in order to get someone into a better place, the next time you come across someone in difficulty, pain, and suffering, offer them some help if you are in the capacity to do so. By doing such things, you will be doing God's will.

This being said here is the story that I felt compelled to share with you guys.

When Jesus gave his famous *"Sermon on the Mount,"* he said, *"Blessed are you who are poor, for yours is the kingdom of God. Blessed are you who hunger now, for you will be satisfied. Blessed are you who weep now, for you will laugh"* (Luke 6: 20-22 NIV).

When I first read this, I couldn't understand it. How could I be blessed if I am poor, tearful, and hungry?

In the Old Testament, there is the story of Joseph, son of Jacob, which helps illustrate what Jesus said and reinforces the power of God. It goes like this:

> Joseph was loved by his father more than his brothers. One night, Joseph had a dream in which he saw himself ruling over his brothers and father. The next morning, he told his family about it. His family members didn't like hearing this, so his brothers tried to kill him. One of the brothers thought better of the scheme and suggested that, instead, they sell him to slave merchants, which is what happened. Joseph was sent to Egypt where he went to work in Potiphar's house. Potiphar was one of Pharaoh's officials.

> Joseph was favored by Potiphar and, because he was a diligent and trustworthy worker, he was quickly promoted. He was also very handsome, so much so that Potiphar's wife lusted after him. She tried to entice him to her bed, but Joseph refused her advances because he was righteous. Potiphar's wife became upset with this rejection and lied to her husband, claiming that Joseph had tried to rape her. Joseph was accused without justice and thrown into jail. He spent more than two years there.

> We can imagine what life must have been like for Joseph, how he must have felt. At one time he lived with his father and brothers and was happy, but then his brothers turned against him and sold him as a servant. Although separated from his father, he

managed to do well in his job, but in honoring his boss, his boss's wife turned against him and his boss believed the lie. Now, here he is … in a prison. We can imagine what the prison was like. Dark, dusty, rats scampering around and un-bathed prisoners making what was bad enough, even worse with their odors. Joseph had also probably gone from having all the food he could eat to not enough.

But even in this horrible place, Joseph was favored. The prison-keeper put Joseph "in charge" of all that went on within the prison. Sometime later, Joseph was released to Pharaoh's house where, after helping the great ruler interpret a dream that would save Egypt during a time of famine, Joseph was elevated in position. Pharaoh said, *"You shall be in charge of my palace, and all my people are to submit to your orders. Only with respect to the throne will I be greater than you"* (Genesis 41:40 NIV).

How awesome is that. After being accused unduly and imprisoned for two years, a couple of years later he found himself with one of the most prestigious jobs in the world. Later on, if you continue reading the story, he confesses the following: (This is the part I want you to "get"),

## "GOD HAS MADE ME FORGET ALL MY TROUBLE"
(Genesis 41:51 NIV).

And this one sentence is one of the main premises this book is written on. That's my entire hope for you regarding your health and your finances—that no matter how bad things are right now with your health or your finances, one day you will forget your current troubles by trusting God and his Word.

Now, if you think back to what Jesus said in His Sermon on the Mount, I believe He was enforcing and reminding people of God's *power*. In the end, when it comes to your health and finances, Jesus has more wisdom, power, and grace than I can ever know, think, or imagine. Having a personal relationship with Jesus Christ is probably the most exhilarating and fulfilling relationship you can ever have.

Ladies and gentlemen, with God, you can do miraculous things with your health and finances. No matter where you are *today*, whether by your own poor choices with food and money or because of something not of your own making such as an illness or losing your job, *God's power* can help you come through any storm to something better. Just as Joseph in time "forgot his troubles" and was reunited with his father and brothers (which was followed by a time of healthy forgiveness), you too can go from unhealthy to healthy … from "broke" or "bankrupt" to wealthy and secure.

That is my hope for you.

May God Bless You
Gee

# ABOUT HEALTHY FINANCIALS, INC

Healthy Financials, Inc. is an accounting and nutritional consulting firm providing services to individuals in need of improvement. Our mission is to "To educate and provide goods and services toward the health and financial improvements of individuals and small businesses." Our specialty and expertise is mostly in individual and small business income taxes. Our staff members have been providing income tax services for more than 7 years.

Our team and associates are composed of Accountants, Enrolled Agents, Certified Public Accountants and Medical Doctors.

Our firm has the resources, experience, and depth of knowledge to offer the following services to both individuals and small businesses. We deliver the service you need in a professional, fast, and cost-efficient manner.

- **Tax Services**
  - ➤ Individual Taxation
  - ➤ Small Business Taxation

- **General Business Consulting**
  - ➤ Start Up Solutions
  - ➤ Management Reporting Solutions

- **Accounting Services**
  - ➤ QuickBooks and Bookkeeping Solutions
  - ➤ Financial Reporting

- **Nutritional Consulting**
  - ➤ Weight Management Solutions

Our office is located in the heart of South Florida in North Miami Beach:

## Address
1820 NE 163rd St, Suite 303
North Miami Beach, FL, 33162

## Phone Numbers
Tel: (305) 788-8195 Fax (305) 224-1855

## Email
healthyfinancials@gmail.com

## Website
www.healthyfinancials.com

# APPENDIX I

# IDEAS AND TOOLS TO HELP IMPROVE YOUR HEALTH

1   Accessories
    1    Backrest Support
    2    HD Sunglasses
    3    7 Day supplemental Boxes
    4    Sleep Mask
    5    Personal Grooming Tools (Tweezers, Nail Clippers, Brushes, Shavers, etc.)
    6    Tooth Brush Covers
    7    Medical History Journal

2   Body Maintenance
    1    Dental Annual Check up
    2    Annual Blood Test: Cholesterol, Diabetes…
    3    Body Massages
    4    Blood Pressure
    5    Primary Care physician Annual Checkup/ Vitals
    6    Vaccines: Hepatitis, Flue Shot, Chickenpox

6  Fitness Classes
   1    Yoga
   2    Pilates
   3    Zumba
   4    Martial Arts
   5    Cycling
   6    Boot Camp
   7    Cardio Kickboxing

7  Foods
   1    Fruits
   2    Vegetables
   3    Nuts & Seeds
   4    Salads
   5    Fish and Shellfish
   6    Beans & Legumes
   7    Herbs and Spices

8  Health products
   1    Vitamins & Dietary Tablets
   2    First-Aid Kits
   3    Cough and Cold Pastilles
   4    Allergy Sinus and Asthma "Mineral Salt Inhaler"
   5    Aromatherapy Inhaler
   6    Muscle Relief Lotions
   7    Whole Body Wrap

9  Memberships
   1    Health Insurance

2 Gym

3 Sports Club (soccer, football, baseball leagues)

4 Association Ex American Diabetes Association

5 Dental Insurance

6 Health Magazine

7 Wellness Center

8 Hobby Clubs and Teams (running, cycling, training)

9 Workshops (writing, poetry, art workshops)

10 Monitor Systems

   1 Digital Thermometer

   2 Calorie Counter (Website or Phone Apps)

   3 Weight Scale

   4 Body Fat and Body Mass Index (BMI) Analyzer

   5 Blood Pressure Monitor

   6 Oximiter for Blood

   7 Activity Tracker Wristband (Synchronizes with smart phone)

11 Nutritional Equipment

   1 Juicer (Juice Extractor)

   2 Slow Cookers

   3 Water Boiler

   4 Mixers

   5 Water Purifier

   6 Toasters & Ovens

   7 Rotisserie Cooker

12 Physical Equipment

   1 Aquatic Equipment (resistance bell, swim mask, swim wear, ear plugs)

2    Helmets for Cycling
3    Jade Heat Infrared Heading Pads
4    Treadmills
5    Elliptical
6    Inversion Table
7    Benches, Dumbbells, Plates

13   Seminars
   1    Spine Disorders
   2    Obesity
   3    Nutrition
   4    Cardio Vascular (Heart Health)
   5    Men's Health or Women's Health
   6    Integrative Medicine (Mind, body and spirit)
   7    Anti-Aging

14   Services
   1    Fitness Instructors
   2    Online Access to Medical Records
   3    Wellness Center (nurse advice help line)
   4    Rehabilitation Center (alcohol and substance  awareness)
   5    Counseling (psychology)
   6    Rape Crisis/Anti- Violence Support Center
   7    Disability (mobility, hearing, vision impairment)
15   Health & Technology
   1    Wellness Phone apps
   2    Advancements in Prosthetic Technology
   3    Mobile Apps (schedule doctor appointments online)
   4    Symptom Checker (Mobile Apps)
   5    Wii Exercise Video Games

# APPENDIX II

# IDEAS AND TOOLS TO HELP IMPROVE YOUR FINANCES

1 Consulting
    1    Asset Protection
    2    Sstate Planning
    3    Financial Planning
    4    Accounting
    5    Annuity Planning
    6    Trust Advising
    7    Pension Calculator
    8    Wealth Management
    9    Portfolio Management
    10    Senior Care Advising
    11    College Planning
    12    Retirement Income Planning
    13    Asset Management
    14    Fund Management

12   Investments
    1    Individual Stocks
    2    Rental Real Estate
    3    Real Estate Investment Trust (REIT)
    4    Index Funds
    5    International Investing
    6    Emerging Market Investing
    7    S&P 500 Companies (large, medium and small caps)
    8    Currency Trading

13   Management and Stewardship
    1    What the Bible Teaches About Money
    2    Biblical Counseling
    3    Principle of Tithing
    4    God is the Owner and Humans are Managers
    5    Planning God's Way
    6    Managing God's Money
    7    Teaching Kids About Money

14   Accounting
    1    Personal Financial Statements
    2    Zero Sum Budget
    3    Cash Flow Planning
    4    Lease vs. Buying
    5    Rent vs. Buying
    6    Finding the right mortgage
    7    Interest Calculator

15  Educational Materials and Resources
    1    Books
    2    DVD
    3    Software
    4    Seminars
    5    Webinars
    6    EBooks
    7    Magazine
    8    Local Public Library
    9    Community Religious Organization
    10   Public Schools
    11   YouTube
    12   Social Media

# THANK YOU

Thank you very much for purchasing this book and taking your time to read it. Hopefully it has been valuable to you and will make a considerable difference your life. I am truly grateful for your time, money and consideration.

I would very much appreciate if you recommend this book to someone that may benefit from the teachings you've just read and also write a good review on Amazon.com and Goodreads.com

Please subscribe to my email list at:

# WWW.HEALTHYFINANCIALS.COM

Printed in the United States
by Brookstream

Printed in the United States
By Bookmasters